DATE

S0-ARO-166

TEXT AND PERFORM

General Editor: Michael Scott

The **series is** designed to introduce sixth-form and under-graduate students to the themes, continuing vitality and performance of major dramatic works. The attention given to production aspects is an element of special importance, responding to the invigoration given to literary study by the work of leading contemporary critics.

The prime aim is to present each play as a vital experience in the mind of the reader – achieved by analysis of the text in relation to its themes and theatricality. Emphasis is accordingly placed on the relevance of the work to the modern reader and the world of today. At the same time, traditional views are presented and appraised, forming the basis from which a creative response to the text can develop.

In each volume, Part One: *Text* discusses certain key themes or problems, the reader being encouraged to gain a stronger perception both of the inherent character of the work and also of variations in interpreting it. Part Two: *Performance* examines the ways in which these themes or problems have been handled in modern productions, and the approaches and techniques employed to enhance the play's accessibility to modern audiences.

A synopsis of the play is given and an outline of its major sources, and a concluding Reading List offers guidance to the student's independent study of the work.

PUBLISHED

IN PREPARATION

RICHARD II

Text and Performance

MALCOLM PAGE

HUMANITIES PRESS INTERNATIONAL, INC.
Atlantic Highlands, NJ

13902647
DLC

1-4-90

First published in 1987 in the United States of America by
HUMANITIES PRESS INTERNATIONAL, INC., Atlantic Highlands, NJ 07716

© Malcolm Page 1987

LIBRARY OF CONGRESS CATALOGING IN PUBLICATION DATA
Page, Malcolm.
    Richard II.
    (Text and performance)
    Bibliography: p.
    Includes index.
    1. Shakespeare, William, 1564–1616. King Richard II.
2. Shakespeare, William, 1564–1616—Stage history—
1950–   . 3. Richard II, King of England, 1367–1400,
in fiction, drama, poetry, etc. I. Shakespeare, William,
1564–1616. King Richard II. II. Title. III. Series.
PR2820.P3   1987   822.3'3   86–18640
ISBN 0–391–03466–9 (pbk.)

PRINTED IN HONG KONG

CONTENTS

Illustrations will be found in Part Two.

CONTENTS

Acknowledgement
Chosen Editions / Text
List of Plots and Figures

PART ONE: TEXT

PART TWO: PERFORMANCE

Illustrations will be found in Part Two.

ACKNOWLEDGEMENTS

My thanks are due to the Archives at the Stratford Festival, Ontario and to the Shakespeare Centre, Stratford-upon-Avon for all their help.

To JONATHAN,
the actor

GENERAL EDITOR'S PREFACE

For many years a mutual suspicion existed between the theatre director and the literary critic of drama. Although in the first half of the century there were important exceptions, such was the rule. A radical change of attitude, however, has taken place over the last thirty years. Critics and directors now increasingly recognise the significance of each other's work and acknowledge their growing awareness of interdependence. Both interpret the same text, but do so according to their different situations and functions. Without the director, the designer and the actor, a play's existence is only partial. They revitalise the text with action, enabling the drama to live fully at each performance. The academic critic investigates the script to elucidate its textual problems, understand its conventions and discover how it operates. He may also propose his view of the work, expounding what he considers to be its significance.

Dramatic texts belong therefore to theatre and to literature. The aim of the 'Text and Performance' series is to achieve a fuller recognition of how both enhance our enjoyment of the play. Each volume follows the same basic pattern. Part One provides a critical introduction to the play under discussion, using the techniques and criteria of the literary critic in examining the manner in which the work operates through language, imagery and action. Part Two takes the enquiry further into the play's theatricality by focusing on selected productions of recent times so as to illustrate points of contrast and comparison in the interpretation of different directors and actors, and to demonstrate how the drama has worked on the modern stage. In this way the series seeks to provide a lively and informative introduction to major plays in their text and performance.

MICHAEL SCOTT

PLOT SYNOPSIS AND SOURCES

I. King Richard II listens to a quarrel between his cousin, Bolingbroke, and Mowbray and, as they cannot agree, orders them to duel. The Duchess of Gloucester tries to persuade John of Gaunt (father of Bolingbroke) to revenge the death of her husband at the hands of Mowbray. When Bolingbroke and Mowbray are about to fight, Richard instead exiles both, Bolingbroke for ten years, changed to six, and Mowbray for life.

II. Gaunt, dying, laments the decline of England during Richard's reign: as soon as he is dead, Richard seizes his wealth and leaves to suppress a rising in Ireland. The Duke of York, the King's uncle, is made Governor. Bolingbroke returns to claim his father's title. He is joined by Northumberland and several others and York submits. Lacking news from Ireland, the royal army disperses.

III. Bolingbroke executes two of Richard's favourites. Richard at last comes back and, after bursts of hope, despairs of his prospects. He confronts Bolingbroke at Flint Castle, and descends to obey Bolingbroke's summons to London. The Queen learns of her husband's fate by overhearing gardeners.

IV. Bolingbroke also faces quarrelsome nobles and the Bishop of Carlisle denounces his seizure of the throne, then is arrested. Richard is formally deposed and forced to give the crown to Bolingbroke, now Henry IV. He refuses when Northumberland demands that he read the accusations against him.

V. Richard and his Queen sadly say goodbye. Aumerle starts plotting to restore Richard to the throne, but his father, York, discovers this. Aumerle successfully pleads with King Henry for forgiveness. Richard, imprisoned in Pomfret (Pontefract) Castle, is visited by a sympathetic groom, then killed by Exton, who believes Henry ordered this. When Exton presents the corpse to Henry, he exiles him and starts mourning Richard.

SOURCES

The question of sources is both simple and complicated. The main source, as for Shakespeare's other histories, is clearly Ralph Holinshed's *Chronicles* (1587), accessible as *Holinshed's Chronicles as used in Shakespeare's Plays*, ed. Richard Hosley (New York, 1968) and elsewhere, and with other sources in *Narrative and Dramatic Sources of Shakespeare*, ed. Geoffrey Bullough, vol. III (1960). Shakespeare may well have consulted several other texts, including Hall's earlier *Chronicles* and the anonymous play *Woodstock*. See, for example, Kenneth Muir, *The Sources of Shakespeare's Plays* (1977), pp. 46–66. Shakespeare *may* have researched with unusual care and then taken pains to harmonise his materials.

PART ONE: TEXT

1 INTRODUCTION

Richard II begins in the middle: no Chorus, as in *Henry V*; no explanatory talk among waiting Gentlemen. This could easily be *Richard II, Part II*, particularly if we know that Richard has already been king for 21 years when the play begins. Instead of any setting of scene and situation, the king is seen presiding while two nobles quarrel cryptically. We cannot tell who is right and who is wrong in the argument, who is lying or whether both are. Our inability to grasp the issues forces our attention on the king, on his way of dealing with troublesome subjects.

Does Shakespeare intend to puzzle spectators with this bitter argument about complicity in the murder of the Duke of Gloucester, the king's uncle? Or does he assume that the first audiences in 1595 brought knowledge lacking in audiences now? Shakespeare here seems to expect spectators to know that Gloucester was killed, directly or indirectly, on the king's orders and that Mowbray is implicated. Audience members who had seen the anonymous play, *Woodstock*, probably staged a little earlier, would know all about the murder of Gloucester. When Richard's involvement is finally mentioned by John of Gaunt, 'Correction lieth in those hands/Which made the fault that we cannot correct' [I ii 4–5], the reference is too oblique to be readily grasped.

The problem of adequately informing audiences of the situation at the start was alleviated at the Bristol Old Vic in 1985 by playing the second scene first, spotlighting Mowbray, Bolingbroke and York when they are named.

Another difficulty initially is that Bolingbroke is also referred to as Hereford (sometimes 'Herford' in the Quarto and Folio texts, which gives the usual pronunciation as two syllables), Mowbray is also Norfolk, John of Gaunt is also Lancaster and the dead Gloucester is also Woodstock (these can give as much initial difficulty as the multiplicity of names in Chekhov's plays). Shakespeare spelt Bolingbroke 'Bullingbrooke' and the recent Riverside and New Cambridge editions have returned to authenticity (but for the final 'e') at the risk of creating confusion. Titles are important: for instance, Bolingbroke on his return in II iii says 'As I was banished, I was banished Hereford;/But as I come, I come for Lancaster' [112–13]. A Duke receives a new title: 'We create . . . Our uncle York Lord Governor of England' [II i 219–20]. Aumerle's title is reduced to a lesser one: 'Aumerle that was; . . . And, madam, you must call him Rutland now' [v ii 41, 43]. Titles matter because the characters 'exist by virtue of their names and titles rather than as individual beings; and like [Richard] express themselves in prescribed forms and set rhetorical figures which mask direct personal response. The being of the man resides in his name. . . . Apart from their formal titles they are nothing' (James Winny, *The Player King*, pp. 48–9). Andrew Gurr stresses the implications of the use of different titles: 'Names work in their context as an index of value and a register of order. . . . When names lose stability, language is equally unstable' (New Cambridge edn, 1984, pp. 33, 34). Nevertheless, prompt copies show that recent productions often deal with the audience's difficulty by changing the text and always using the better-known name.

This opening scene shows us the king and the nobility, an all-male world. The young king, with only old John of Gaunt as a counsellor, is faced with disrespectful yet powerful courtiers. Eloquent words half-conceal both the issues and the true nature of the men. Procedures are formal, with kneeling and the throwing down of gages: the play will feature dignified ritual more than action throughout. The quarrel is not resolved: Richard finally orders the duel, which will provide 'justice' [203]. We know we are in a medieval world, remote to the first Elizabethan audiences of the play, as well as to us. Formality just conceals the actual passionate hates – the play's underlying themes of power and principles are already emerging.

The first scene is a formal court occasion with the stage filled with 'other nobles' and 'attendants'; the king probably wears his crown. The second scene is domestic, with only two characters. This is the pattern, the alternation of formal and informal scenes, and of long and short ones. Though Dover Wilson writes that it 'should be played throughout as ritual' (New Shakespeare, [Cambridge, 1939], p. xiii) some scenes are clearly casual and small scale.

Structurally, the play moves forward in four parts: Richard as king [I i to III iii]; the transference of power [III iii and III iv]; the deposition [IV i] and Bolingbroke as king [v]. While the play advances from one king to his successor, events are repeated so the drama can almost be seen as circular. In the first act Richard struggles to deal with his violently-quarrelling nobles and in IV i Bolingbroke has to cope with exactly the same problem. *Richard II* begins with a king to some degree responsible for a murder and ends with the new king also partly responsible for the killing of his predecessor. Richard is faced with plots and rebellions; so is Bolingbroke in both v iii and v vi.

The verse of the opening scene from time to time switches to rhyme [41–7, 82–3, 122–3, 150–1, 154–95, 200–5]. While some argue that these lines show the characters' prepared speeches, in contrast to spontaneity, the point seems more Shakespeare experimenting, wondering whether the tradition of rhyme is compatible with his kind of tragedy.

This first scene introduces such themes as pride in being English [66, 94]. The four elements are all mentioned in the opening lines: 'deaf as the sea, hasty as fire' [19], 'the heavens, envying earth's good hap' [23] and 'sky' [41]. The continuing pattern is that 'Richard, the sun-king of fire, contends with Bullingbrook, the flood. Their stormy conflict drowns Richard's fire in the water of tears and changes Bullingbrook into the sun' (Gurr, New Cambridge edn, p. 23). Richard's end is burial, in earth. Most conspicuous in scene one is blood (nine mentions, and 'bleed' and 'bleeding') and the humour of blood combines fire and water. Blood connotes the noble birth of Richard and the aristocrats at court and also the blood of murder, conflict and battle, the fear of bloodshed staining the fair earth of England.

2 RICHARD: MAN AND KING

Act I – Act II 1: Richard's Mistakes and Crimes

The opening exchange of the play between king and subject
shows the traditional and appropriate relationship. Richard
reminds John of Gaunt of 'oath and band' ('band' is a form
of 'bond') in the second line and Gaunt answers 'my liege'
[7] (Richard is entitled to receive allegiance, even from an
elderly member of the royal family). A violent quarrel, stage-
managed by the apparently all-powerful monarch, follows.

Richard faces a difficult problem in resolving the quarrel.
Bolingbroke is his cousin and a member of the royal family,
another descendant of Edward III. Mowbray knows of
Richard's involvement in the murder of Gloucester and could
incriminate the king. Bolingbroke and Mowbray are both
noblemen and invoke a tradition of chivalry which challenges
the royal authority Richard wants to exercise. Bolingbroke
invokes 'all the rites of knighthood' [76] and Mowbray
similarly:

> By that sword I swear
> Which gently laid my knighthood on my shoulder,
> I'll answer thee in any fair degree
> Or chivalrous design of knightly trial   [78–81]

The old chivalric code of the nobility is set against the new
style absolutism of the king.

Richard, as king and man, conducts himself well at first,
questioning carefully in five of his first six speeches, asserting
his impartiality [115], promising freedom of speech [123]
and seeking a peaceful solution: 'Let's purge this choler
without shedding blood' [153]. He spoils his effect by adding
a half-hearted, self-conscious joke, 'Our doctors say this is no
month to bleed' [157].

Derek Jacobi, who played the king for television, explains
the actor's difficulty at the beginning of the play: 'Shakespeare
hasn't really given any indication from Richard's point of

view that he actually saw that the murder [of Gloucester] was done. If you're playing Richard you have to decide "Did I do it or didn't I?" and inform the lines from there. The first scene is frightfully difficult – it's so sketchy for Richard. He doesn't say very much and what he says is frightfully kingly and public, but the man's got a lot to hide and a lot to lose and a lot to gain from the situation, and it's completely understated by Shakespeare' (BBC TV edn, pp. 22–3).

Richard completely changes his mind and orders trial by combat instead, contradicting his aim of avoiding bloodshed. On the personal level, he shows his impulsive side. On the political level, he has abandoned his authority and permitted the old chivalric practice.

Richard, the king, and a medieval king, 'is in perfect accord with this pageant-like ritual. He is the spire of court ceremony; he is on display as an incarnation of the anointed king' (Travis Bogard, 'Shakespeare's Second Richard', *PMLA*, 70, 1955, p. 202). Already we start to doubt whether the man wielding all this authority deserves to, whether he is wielding it intelligently.

Not only is the switch to decision by duel arbitrary, this way of settling disputes may be questioned by Elizabethans as well as by ourselves. Diane Borstein notes the 16th-century argument between anti-duel Christian humanists and pro-duel supporters of a neochivalric cult of honour. She aligns the writer with the former, so that, by the end of I i, 'Shakespeare shows the king to have an attitude that is presumptuous, unjust, unpatriotic, and un-English. . . . Richard expects God to perform a miracle on demand. On the contrary, John of Gaunt states that it is necessary to leave a quarrel "to the will of heaven/Who, when they see the hours ripe on earth,/Will rain hot vengeance on offenders' heads" [I ii 6–8]' ('Trial by Combat and Official Irresponsibility in *Richard II*,' *Shakespeare Studies*, 8, 1975, pp. 131–41).

When the day of the duel arrives [I iii], Richard presides with dignity and formality, until, at the last possible moment, he halts the combat. He delays so long, in fact, that perhaps he seeks a dramatic effect. Again he has abruptly changed his mind, or, worse, planned his effect from the start, as John Palmer suspects: 'For him the whole elaborate to-do, with its heralds and trumpets, solemn appeals to heaven, ceremonious farewells and heroic attitudes, was matter for a May morning. He knows that these doughty champions are inflating themselves to no purpose. The actor playing Richard should watch them with a twinkle, impishly awaiting the moment when he will knock the bottom out of all these political high jinks. . . . The whole scene is in the nature of a practical joke' (*Political Characters of Shakespeare*, [London, 1945], p. 131).

Though the way in which the duel is stopped may be theatrical, the motive appears worthy: 'That our kingdom's earth should not be soiled/With that dear blood which it hath fostered' [125–6]. Even here, Richard may be insincere: 'The tortuously long sentence [123–39], the involved construction, the piled-up relative clauses, the pronouns with ambiguous antecedents, the excess of hyphenated adjectives, all go to show how a poetically gifted but mentally dishonest and frightened man expresses himself when he opens his mouth and lets what will come come. Examine the speech, and it falls to pieces like the pack of – words it is' (Harold Goddard, *The Meaning of Shakespeare*, [Chicago, 1951], p. 151).

Richard follows with more questionable decisions, blunders, misjudgements. He exiles Bolingbroke for ten years, Mowbray for life: unequal punishments for no sound reason. Alec Guinness in the role dwelt with 'conscious pleasure' on the 'sly slow hours' and 'the dateless limit of thy dear exile' [150–1]. When Mowbray protests, 'Richard's tone changes to summary condemnation. Richard is, in fact, making a poem out of the idea of perpetual banishment. Of [Mowbray] as a person he simply does not think at all' (Harold Hobson, *Theatre*, 1948, p. 168). As Mowbray starts to go, Richard – impulsive again – demands that both men swear an oath that they never will meet 'To plot, contrive, or complot any ill/'Gainst us, our state, our subjects, or our land' [189–90] – which might just be putting an idea into their minds! A fourth startlingly abrupt decision follows: because John of Gaunt looks so 'grieved' and 'sad' [209] at the exiling of his son, the sentence is cut to six years.

In the next scene, for the first time Richard is off-duty, with friends. His first question is about Bolingbroke's departure. He shows no interest in Mowbray and we may start to suspect that he was less impartial than he claimed to be. Richard then describes Bolingbroke's 'courtship to the common people' [24]. While this may be very calculating on the part of the ambitious Bolingbroke, common people ourselves, we wonder about a king who speaks contemptuously of his subjects as 'slaves' [27]. 'Poor craftsmen,' 'oyster-wenches' and 'draymen' [28–32] are Richard's countrymen too, though rarely mentioned in the play. Then Green has to prompt Richard to remember 'the rebels which stand out in Ireland' [38] and Richard makes what may well be yet another impulsive decision to lead the army against the rebels himself. By now, late in the first act, we are dubious about Richard's character and the quality of his decision-making. He moves to more overtly immoral acts, tax-farming and 'blank charters' for use against the rich. When news comes that John of Gaunt is grievous sick, Richard's response is startlingly callous: may he die quickly so that his wealth can be used to help finance his war. However strong Richard's sense of the grandeur of kingship, he has few abilities in dealing with everyday political and personal realities and his morality is also severely questioned.

Richard visits the dying Gaunt in II i and, criticised by him, speaks brutally to the old man, 'a lunatic lean-witted fool' [115]. As soon as Gaunt's death is reported to him, Richard illegally seizes his lands and goods, acting against the very laws of inheritance which gave him the throne, stating 'The ripest fruit first falls, and so doth he./His time is spent, our pilgrimage must be' [II i 153–4]. This is flippant doggerel. He continues 'Now for our Irish wars': his immediate pilgrimage is not a religious one, but in a dubious cause. When York protests at Richard taking Gaunt's inheritance, he is rudely dismissive: 'Why, uncle, what's the matter?' [186]. Two minutes later – unpredictable and perverse again – the king appoints York as Lord Governor during his absence in Ireland. At worst, this is indifference to the fate of England; at best, a political gamble, an attempt to ensure York's continued loyalty. Richard sets off for Ireland, a king whose every act has shown him unworthy to be a king.

Richard is away in Ireland for a time. We never learn
whether taking command personally is responsible or – given
the troubles he leaves behind in England – irresponsible.
That his decision to go is a whim casts doubt on the
expedition. Neither do we ever hear whether or not he is
victorious. He returns to an England occupied by Bolingbroke.
He may return a changed man, as John Neville, playing the
role at the Old Vic in 1955, found: 'The difficulty for the
actor playing the King is the fact that there are two different
characters. As he appears in the first part of the play; then,
he goes away to Ireland, there's a pause, and he's not on a
great deal. Then he comes back to England and appears to
be a very different kind of character. We quite blatantly
made no attempt to link the two; he came back from Ireland
a different man, that is what he was, and that's the way we
played it' (*Acting in the Sixties*, ed. Hal Burton, [BBC, 1970],
p. 101).

III 111: *Unconditional Surrender*

In III i Bolingbroke acted like a ruler in ordering executions;
and at the end of III ii Richard discharged his followers. The
rising Bolingbroke meets the falling Richard at Flint Castle.
As audience we wonder how they will behave in a situation
new and awkward for both, reversing the power-structure
seen in I iii, when the king banished Bolingbroke. Bolingbroke
is supported by the tough Northumberland, York, still uneasy
at changing sides, and Percy, a new arrival, showing the
rebels' strength growing. King Richard's supporters are
Aumerle and three men who do not speak in the scene: the
Bishop of Carlisle (the Church supports Richard; his
opponents do not include any churchmen), Scroop and
Salisbury. Bolingbroke is outside the castle as though laying
siege. Richard is within the 'lime and stone . . . of that
ancient castle' [26, 31] but the battlements are 'tattered' [52]
(but the word *may* mean 'having pointed projections'). In
staging the scene, Bolingbroke and his party are first separate
from the castle and his army marches across the stage [51].
Bolingbroke's trumpets outside are answered by Richard's

from inside. When Richard appears he is on the balcony of
the stage. By line 176 the space is no longer outside the
castle, but in its lower courtyard. Richard's 'Down, down I
come' [178] in an Elizabethan theatre would require him to
go out of sight to descend a staircase; in modern theatres
more effectively he can stay in view, walking slowly down as
he speaks.

Bolingbroke at the start appears totally assured, while not
intending unnecessary disrespect to Richard. When he says
of the castle, 'Royally? Why, it contains no king' [23] he
probably does not know Richard is close, though the Marlowe
Society Actor's firm intonation* shows that Bolingbroke
no longer recognises Richard as king, any more than
Northumberland has done at line 6. Bolingbroke's public
message to Richard is of allegiance, on two conditions: 'My
banishment repealed/And lands restored again' [40–1]. Keith
Michell speaks these lines respectfully but the Marlowe Society
actor leaves doubt about Bolingbroke's sincerity: maybe he,
as well as Richard, is an actor. His threat, 'I'll use the
advantage of my power/And lay the summer's dust with
showers of blood' [42–3] is much fiercer than Michell's; he
commands 'Go signify as much' [49]; his 'Let's march
without the noise of threatening drum' [51] is calculating,
not an honest sign that he wants peace. Bolingbroke as usual
is quite direct, while Richard loves words and images for
their own sake.

Richard appears splendidly dressed, wearing his crown and
probably a sun emblem above – a scene especially effective
in open-air performance at Ludlow Castle. He looks 'like a
king', as York observes [68], but it is 'so fair a show' [71].

---

*Here and later I draw on three recordings of the play. Sir John Gielgud's
performance is preserved in the Caedmon Shakespeare Recording Society version of
1960. The impressive cast includes Keith Michell as Bolingbroke, Leo McKern as
John of Gaunt, Michael Hordern as York, Jeremy Brett as Mowbray and Harold
Lang as Northumberland. The other full-length version, recorded by Cambridge
students of the Marlowe Society with some professionals in 1958 for London
records, is well-spoken, but the Richard is under-characterised. Michael Redgrave
plays Richard on the abridged one-record Living Shakespeare version, with Nigel
Davenport as Bolingbroke, and Hordern again John of Gaunt. Spoken Arts has an
abridged text with Christopher Casson and Fred Johnson and Allegro one with
Robert Harris and John Ruddock.

Richard as usual is attractive but superficial: while
looking like a king he does not behave or govern like one. Yet
Richard's first response is formal and convincing; he assumes
the sanctity of the monarch as a law of nature. He describes
the aid given him by God, then breaks off when he sees
Bolingbroke and rushes ahead of the actual situation in
assuming battle is intended. Bolingbroke contrasted 'blood'
and 'crimson' with 'green', 'grassy' England [43–50] and
Richard develops this at greater length: 'purple', 'bleeding',
'scarlet' and 'blood' versus 'flower' and 'grass' [94–100].

Northumberland replies formally in his role as envoy.
Carefully, he draws on traditional reverences, while urging
subject's rights, pointing out that Bolingbroke is also of royal
descent ('by the royalties of both your bloods,' [97]). As
Northumberland has just refused to kneel to Richard, we
may be sceptical when he says Bolingbroke begs 'on his
knees' [114].

King Richard immediately accepts Bolingbroke's demands,
surprisingly. His next words are as an intimate friend to
Aumerle, who advises playing for time. Richard invokes God,
meaningful for him, not a thoughtless oath:

> O God, O God, that e'er this tongue of mine,
> That laid the sentence of dread banishment
> On yon proud man, should take it off again   [132–4]

> Must he lose
> The name of King? A God's name, let it go.   [145–6]

(Brian Bedford, who played the part at Stratford, Ontario, in
1983, remarks: 'The relation between Richard II and God is
probably the most important in that play. Being stripped of
everything, he begins to see who he is, and consequently
begins to see what God is'; Keith Garebian, 'The Dramatic
Art of Brian Bedford', *Performing Arts in Canada*, Winter 1983,
p. 36). Richard sinks into misery, switching to the first
person singular, 'O that I were as great/As is my grief' [136–
37], admittedly speaking only to Aumerle. Richard's moan is
interrupted by Aumerle's effort to force him back to the
urgency of the situation, 'Northumberland comes back from
Bolingbroke' [142].

Incredibly, Richard gives up everything. He has not been asked to abdicate but states that he submits to deposition. By assuming this, he causes it: he has lost his grip on reality. Four lines of renouncing the throne lead to thirteen lines of lament, addressed to Northumberland, the least sympathetic person there. Aumerle weeps and Richard develops a conceit about tears for ten more lines, till laughter from someone finally reminds him of the situation. His tone is forceful as he speaks publicly but he has submitted to 'King Bolingbroke' [173]. His tone is cold and contemptuous: we may find that he sounds foolish.

Northumberland, now confident in his disrespect, coolly asks the king to come down to meet his visitor. Richard obeys, with a loud, passionate lament, almost the owls' shriek he mentions (by both Gielgud and Redgrave), 'like a frantic man', in Northumberland's phrase [185].

Richard comes down literally and symbolically, yet the balance of power is still shaky. Cautiously, Bolingbroke kneels and orders his followers to do so. They may be kneeling to the crown rather than to the wearer, and Nigel Davenport (Bolingbroke to Redgrave's Richard) puts irony into 'my gracious lord' [189]. Bolingbroke may indeed be deliberately overdoing a calculated pseudo-respect when he repeats this form of address [196] and just after, uses 'my most redoubted lord' [198].

Richard here for once manages to speak briefly and to the point, touching the crown as he tells Bolingbroke 'Your heart is up, I know,/*Thus high at least*,' [194–5]. Bolingbroke is still negotiating with the ambiguous 'I come but for mine own' [196]; Richard has given up, 'I am yours and all' [197] – self-pitying, self-dramatising and first person singular. At this point – unlike most of the deposition scene – Bolingbroke looks the worthier human being, as well as the more impressive leader. Richard retrieves dignity when he consoles the weeping York (contrasting with his indulging Aumerle's tears a little earlier) and accepts the realities of Bolingbroke's determination (he knows 'the strongest and the surest way to get,' [201]) and larger army: 'do we must what force will have us do' [207]. Richard, still wearing the crown, leads the way out, but he is escorted, almost a prisoner. He may

manage a little last joke, as well as weary acceptance, with
'Then I must not say no' [209].

Richard can be seen in this episode as so much a medieval
monarch, so dependent on ceremony and tradition, that he
turns his submission into a ceremony, appearing in all his
glory on high, an English *roi soleil*, then descending so
spectacularly that he distracts us from seeing him as merely
obeying the orders of Northumberland. Though Richard may
be governed by the nature of kingship, a particularised
human being is drawn for us.

If Richard is perceived in this scene more as an individual
than as a king, or rather as an individual inadequately
coping with the role of king, we will prefer Ernest Dowden's
view;

> His feelings live in the world of phenomena, and altogether fail
> to lay hold of things as they are; they have no consistency and no
> continuity. . . . He is at the mercy of every chance impulse and
> transitory mood. He has a kind of artistic relation to life, without
> being an artist. . . . Richard, to whom all things are unreal, has a
> fine feeling for 'situations.' Without true kingly strength or
> dignity, he has a fine feeling for the royal situation. Without any
> making real to himself what God or what death is, he can put
> himself, if need be, in the appropriate attitude towards God and
> towards death. Instead of comprehending things as they are, and
> achieving heroic deeds, he satiates his heart with the grace, the
> tenderness, the beauty or the pathos of situations. Life is to
> Richard a show, a succession of images; and to put himself into
> accord with the aesthetic requirements of his position is Richard's
> first necessity. He is equal to playing any part gracefully which
> he is called upon by circumstances to enact. But when he has
> exhausted the aesthetic satisfaction to be derived from the
> situations of his life, he is left with nothing further to do
> (*Shakspere, A Critical Study of His Mind and Art* [London, 1875],
> pp. 194–5).

This description catches the Richard who sees the loss of his
kingdom as the occasion for luxuriating in self-pity.

The key issue in Richard's failure in this scene is that he
gives up, not only without a fight, but without taking time to
bargain. In part this is the arrogance of a king, even of a king

with few followers left, refusing to bargain with a subject. He does not seek time to think or seek advice; he surrenders his kingdom to a man who claims he only wants his inheritance. This is folly and stupidity; Richard is unable to handle a situation he has never faced before.

IV 1: Deposition

Act IV contains Bolingbroke's assumption of the throne and Richard's renunciation of kingship. This scene too is a formal ceremony, in parliament. York begins it

> Great Duke of Lancaster, I come to thee
> From plume-plucked Richard, who with willing soul
> Adopts thee heir, and his high sceptre yields
> To the possession of thy royal hand.
> Ascend his throne, descending now from him,
> And long live Henry, fourth of that name!

Bolingbroke goes to sit on the throne, 'In God's name I'll ascend the regal throne' [107–13]. The ceremony is at once interrupted, with a protest by the Bishop of Carlisle. He is silenced and Richard brought in. Richard stages a symbolic pantomime, with Bolingbroke's hand and his on the crown. As Alec Guinness played it: 'Balancing it lightly in his fingers, an inch from the usurper's nose, he says gently and with infinite scorn: "Here, cousin – *seize* the crown" [181]. The eyes spoke most compellingly as the actor dwelt, with pensive irony, on the long "ee" of "seize"' (Kenneth Tynan, *A View of the English Stage*, [London, 1975], p. 62). When Bolingbroke asks 'Are you contented to resign the crown?' Richard answers 'Ay, no. No, ay' [199–200], the essence of his indecision, his 'To be or not to be'. As Richard knows the reality of Bolingbroke's power, the wavering is part of his calculated performance. Finally he hands over crown and sceptre:

> I give this heavy weight from off my head,
> And this unwieldy sceptre from my hand,

The pride of kingly sway from out my heart.
With mine own tears I wash away my balm
                              (balm = consecrated oil)
With mine own hands I give away my crown,
With mine own tongue deny my sacred state,
With mine own breath release all duteous oaths.   [203-9]

Richard turns his deposition into a kind of unholy rite, a reverse coronation; as he leaves, Bolingbroke announces, 'On Wednesday next we solemnly proclaim/Our coronation' [318-19].

'The Form and Order of Her Majesty's Coronation' in 1953 is remarkably similar to the 14th-century coronation. The ceremony begins with the Recognition, when the Archbishop of Canterbury says: 'Sirs, I here present unto you Queen Elizabeth, your undoubted Queen: Wherefore all you who are come this day to do your homage and service. Are you willing to do the same?' 'The people signify their willingness and joy, by loud and repeated acclamations, all with one voice crying out "God save Queen Elizabeth".' Then, the spiritual climax, the Archbishop anoints the Queen with holy oil, in the form of a cross, on the palms, breast and crown of the head: 'Be thy head anointed with holy Oil: as kings, priests, and prophets were anointed: And as Solomon was anointed king by Zadok the priest and Nathan the prophet, so be thou anointed, blessed, and consecrated Queen over the Peoples, whom the Lord thy God hath given thee to rule and govern.' Next, the Queen is arrayed in the white Colobium Sindonis and the golden Supertunica. The Garter Principal King of Arms explains this part: these 'vestments so closely resembling those of a bishop that some writers in the Middle Ages have argued that coronation makes the sovereign a "mixed person", both layman and priest.' Finally, the Queen receives the orb, the sceptre, 'the ensign of kingly power and justice', the rod and lastly the crown.

Returning to Richard's deposition, having surrendered the regalia, Northumberland demands that he read the accusations against him. Again the ceremony does not go as planned: Richard refuses to read. Richard, impulsive earlier, is calculating here. Ian Richardson comments: 'It is perhaps unkind to imagine Richard preparing for his last great public scene, again as an actor, but it's irresistible. I am sure he dressed with care to present just the right image of humility and distress. He certainly pulls out all the stops when he renounces for ever his sovereignty before his cousin and the assembled lords. This is his swan-song and he is going to make sure that none of his audience forgets it. He is magnificent, and no doubt deeply embarrasing to Henry, who hardly speaks throughout the scene. Richard accuses the assembled company of betraying him, as Christ was betrayed. It becomes plain that this is the seed he wants to sow. However and whenever he dies, after this, it will be as a sacrificial victim, and Henry will be – at best – Pontius Pilate' [238–41] (*Shakespeare in Perspective*, I, ed. Roger Sales, p. 44).

Richard comes to control the ceremony when he asks for a mirror and stages a second symbolic pantomime. He claims he wants it as a means to self-knowledge: 'I'll read enough/When I do see the very book indeed/Where all my sins are writ; and that's myself' [272–4]. Mirrors are richly ambiguous. They tell the truth, yet Elizabethan crystal glasses are murky enough to be misleading, and the word in the text is 'glass', usually transparent. Further, only the vain, seeking flattery, make much use of mirrors. At this moment the image of himself that Richard has had all his life is being questioned and he hopes the glass will reveal the depths of his misery. Instead, it lies to him, showing the outward semblance, not what he believes to be the inner truth.

Redgrave and the Marlowe Society actor begin with a strong, commanding 'Give me that glass' [275] and remain in control asking the five rhetorical questions. Gielgud, on the other hand, breaks down in his distress. Northumberland's demands infuriate him and his high-flown line, 'Fiend, thou tormentst me ere I come to hell' [269] is sincere. He is genuinely surprised that his change in status is not reflected in a change in his face. The first two questions are to himself, the remaining three directed to his onstage audience, forcing them to realise what they are doing, to an ex-king and to a

man. He continues, wonderingly, is this *really* the same face
which employed ten thousand men and 'like the sun' made
beholders wink. A moment earlier he had recognised that not
only was he no longer the sun but that the usurper had
become 'the sun of Bolingbroke' [260].

The questions lead to the flamboyant gesture of smashing
the glass: David Warner, at Stratford-upon-Avon in 1964,
punched out the glass with his fist, clearly hurting himself.
Richard points what is the 'moral' [289] for him: 'How soon
my sorrow hath destroyed my face' [290], the most unhappy
line in the scene in Gielgud's reading. Sorrow has not
destroyed his face: he has a kind of control in being able to
break the representation of his face. Being easily broken, it
shows the brittleness of his former image. Pretending rejection
of his old self in destroying the mirror, he continues his
pattern of histrionic gestures. The destruction of the mirror-
image of Richard's face anticipates the destruction of the
man. (This commentary on the significance of the mirror
episode draws on Peter Ure, 'The Looking-Glass of *Richard
II*,' *Philological Quarterly*, 34, 1955, pp. 219–24, and Janette
Dillon, *Shakespeare and the Solitary Man*, [London, 1981], ch. 5.)

The Marlowe Society Richard speaks fast, quite decisive
till the final line of the speech. Redgrave appears to have
planned the whole performance, down to relishing his little
wordplay of 'Is this the *face* which *faced* so many follies,/
That was at last out*faced* by Bolingbroke?' [284–5].

Bolingbroke, weary and impatient in his two preceding
speeches, comments quietly, 'The shadow of your sorrow
hath destroyed/The shadow of your face' [291–2]. Nigel
Davenport here enjoys both the words which echo Richard's
final line and his use of 'shadow' in two senses, literal and
metaphorical. The other actors make the remark a matter-of-
fact one. Bolingbroke is ostensibly sympathising with Richard,
commiserating with his grief. 'To Richard the remark seems
to be a sympathetic remark, and so he takes up its surface
meaning. But actually Bolingbroke means something else.
. . . He knows the king won't understand it. . . . When he
says "The shadow of your sorrow", he really means "The
unreality of your sorrow". . . . Your false sorrow has destroyed
your false, playerly face. Bolingbroke is telling Richard that

his sorrow is as unreal as the rest of his public persona'
(John Barton, *Playing Shakespeare* [London, 1984], pp. 122–3).
If Bolingbroke speaks with this double meaning, he has
some measure of control and is not out-manoeuvred by
Richard. Bolingbroke could not point to insincerity when
opposed by Gielgud's heartbroken Richard.

V v: Death

Richard's moving, poetic farewell to his Queen follows [v i]
and he is next seen imprisoned in Pomfret Castle, with a long
and complex soliloquy. For the first time without a stage
audience, he has no role to play and thus is forced to a kind
of confrontation with himself. This has been highly praised:
'In [Richard's] final despair and failure, his mind is thrown
back on pure contemplation and he sinks on to the restful
sweetness of impersonal and wandering thought. In so doing,
he finds that he has made a small world of his own: which
state is now exactly analogous to the creative consciousness
which gives birth to poetry' (G. Wilson Knight, *The Imperial
Theme*, 3rd edn, [London, 1951], p. 351). Though Richard
begins by trying hard to be content with this freedom of the
imagination, he cannot be [32]. Even being king of his own
mind is difficult. Perhaps, though, this is the human
condition, that no man is pleased in life, eased only by death
[40–1] – ironically, his own is closer than he knows. He is
'but man' [39], no longer a king. Has Richard here been able
to free himself from the burden of kingship, since its powers
and responsibilities are lost? He continues to wrestle with
painful adjusting to being an ex-king. Music brings him to
self-knowledge: 'I wasted time' [49]; deep meditation on time
follows. He 'dwells on the lack of proportion, of measured
rhythm, in his reign as it is set against his "true time", the
time he ought to have kept. . . . Richard knows he has
violated natural and political order. . . . He reiterates his
painful sense of being at the mercy of forces beyond him. But
the difference between this and his previous expressions of
helplessness is that now he knows it is his own fault' (Robert
L. Montgomery, Jr, 'The Dimensions of Time in *Richard II*,'

Shakespeare Studies, 4, 1968, pp. 82–3). The harmony of music is 'specially perceived in the field of human relations. Time is also the times, that is to say the age with its characteristics of temper and spirit depending upon social life. It is this social sense of the word that Richard has in mind when he speaks of the "concord of (his) state and time" and regrets that he "had not an ear to hear (his) true time broke" [47–8]. The harmony is one not of sounds but of men' (Michel Grivelet, 'Shakespeare's "War with Time": The Sonnets and *Richard II*,' *Shakespeare Survey*, 23, 1970, p. 75). Richard reverts for a moment to the self-pity of the third and fourth acts with 'sighs and tears and groans' [57]. His mind inevitably turns again to Bolingbroke and his futile anger is directed against the music. Abruptly, he blesses the musician because he thinks he is playing for love of Richard.

Richard here tries to adjust to his change in status and to life in jail; he has still not found peace. Harold Toliver finds Richard's creation of a mental kingdom and his view of time as 'extravagant' and 'ineffectual' ('Shakespeare and the Abyss of Time', *JEGP*, 64, 1965, p. 242. On the soliloquy, see also John Baxter, *Shakespeare's Poetic Styles* pp. 136–43). When he says 'I wasted time' is he repenting idleness and listening to flatterers or is he wishing that he had fought against Bolingbroke? Richard Pasco sees no resolution here: 'Richard's tragedy was that he never actually discovered himself' (Barton, *Playing Shakespeare*, p. 122). On the other hand, Graham Holderness sees Richard as satisfied because now his task is one that he can achieve: 'The prison is a world without people, a kingdom without subjects, which he can fill with his own personality: he can be both ruler and ruled. At last Richard's imagination and will are supreme – now his kingdom has been reduced to the confines of his own mind' ('Shakespeare's History: *Richard II*,' *Literature and History*, 7, 1981, p. 18). The imprisoned Richard is wiser: the Richard seen earlier in the play was not capable of such speculations. He has become, through misfortunes, a better man, though much too late to change him to a good king. In this soliloquy he more than once attains a subdued, sad acceptance, then breaks off suddenly, rejecting the consolations of such a state of mind.

The Marlowe Society actor offers a wise, balanced philosopher here. 'Nor I, nor any man that but man is,/With nothing shall be pleased till he be eased/With being nothing' [39–41] is made to sound profound. He is stirred only on the one line where anger is unmistakable, 'This music mads me' [61].

Michael Redgrave's reading is much more varied. He is a trifle amused at the inevitable failure of his first flight of mind, 'I cannot do it' [5], then enjoys his achievement of forcing his thoughts to 'people this little world' [9]. When his mind turns to his 'ragged prison walls' [21], he is irritated, and bitter when he comes to name Bolingbroke [37]. Though the music he hears is cheerful, it drives him to passionate fury, 'This music mads me'. He recovers to bring out forcefully the contrast between love and the 'all-*hating* world' [66].

Gielgud reveals all the contrasting feelings in the scene, guided by the contradiction of 'I cannot do it. Yet I'll hammer it out' [5]. He is slow and thoughtful, close to a laugh at the chance that 'in this thought they find a kind of ease' [28]. He changes at line 37, furious when Bolingbroke comes to mind. The sound of music – sweet rather than bright – delights him; that he stands fooling here [60] exasperates him; he screams in self-contempt when 'this music mads me'. Gielgud's interpretation requires agitated pacing and sudden movement; the Marlowe Society approach calls for a man sitting, quiet and thoughtful.

Richard has shown himself increasingly unworthy and unscrupulous from the beginning of the play to the seizure of Gaunt's wealth in ii i. At some point between his return from Ireland in iii ii and the end of the deposition scene our sympathies swing to him as he is the underdog, though our sympathy is always troubled by the extent of his self-pity. Pitiable in his farewell to the Queen (v i), he may have acquired wisdom in his prison solilioquy. Whatever his faults, even in their medieval dog-eat-dog world, he does not deserve death (he only banishes his enemies: the killing of Gloucester was offstage and before the play). If the last two scenes are to affect us, Richard the suffering human being matters to us, so his killing of two of his murderers is a belated burst of heroism.

However, one critic, Harold Goddard, despises Richard even in his last moment; 'It is just the reflex action of a man without self-control in the presence of death, as little willed as the galvanic twitching of a frog's leg. It is a fury of desperation pure and simple, a particularly ignominious and ironic end for a king who pretended to believe that everything from stones to angels would come to his rescue in the hour of need' (*The Meaning of Shakespeare*, [Chicago, 1951], p. 159).

During the deposition scene Richard had audaciously compared himself to Christ:

> Did they not sometime cry 'All hail!' to me?
> So Judas did to Christ. But He in twelve
> Found truth in all but one; I, in twelve thousand, none.
> [IV i 169–71]

At Stratford, Connecticut, in 1968 Richard was seen as Christ, or a Christian martyr, at the moment of his death: he was stabbed with his arms outstretched in a crucifixion attitude, the light of a halo round his head.

Richard as actor

Richard II sees himself as a performer, centre stage, when he submits at Flint Castle and when he deflects attention from the new king with his business with the crown and the mirror at his deposition.

Shakespeare at several points reminds us that we are seeing a play performed. 'I *play* the torturer', says Scroop bringing bad news to Richard [III ii 198]. After the deposition, the Abbot of Westminster observes 'A woeful pageant have we here beheld' [IV i 320]. York describes the way the crowd turned its attention from Richard to the new king:

> As in a theatre the eyes of men,
> After a well graced actor leaves the stage,
> Are idly bent on him that enters next,
> Thinking his prattle to be tedious: [V ii 23–6]

When the Duchess follows York to plead for the life of her
son, King Henry comments lightly:

> Our scene is altered from a serious thing,
> And now changed to 'The Beggar and the King'.   [v iii 78–9]

While Richard in his last soliloquy in prison realises 'Thus
play I in one person many people' [v v 31]. Richard is an
actor and knows it; we watch a play in a theatre.

3   BOLINGBROKE AND YORK

Bolingbroke is outwardly straightforward, a bluff and hearty
figure. Commentators use such adjectives as matter-of-fact,
cool, level-headed, practical, resolute, pragmatic, vigorous,
uncomplicated. Compared to Richard, he uses few words.
Exiled, Gaunt asks him 'To what purpose dost thou hoard
thy words?' and he replies 'I have too few to take my leave of
you' [i iii 253, 255]. During the deposition Richard addresses
his as 'silent king' [iv i 289].

   Some hints point to a more calculating, more ambitious
man. He invokes 'the glorious worth of my descent' [i i 107],
the same ancestry as Richard's, entitling him to impose
justice. His father offers ambiguous consolation as he goes
into exile: 'Think not the King did banish thee,/But thou the
King' [i iii 279–80]: imagine that you were the more powerful,
making the decision. Bolingbroke is calculating when he tells
his friends

> I count myself in nothing else so happy
> As in a soul remembering my good friends;
> And as my fortune ripens with thy love
> It shall be still thy true love's recompense   [ii iii 46–9]

Which means 'I'll reward you when I've won.' When he
justifies executing Bushy and Green [iii i 1–30], ostensibly he
argues the cause of Richard and the Queen; equally, he
argues his own cause here.

Once Bolingbroke is king, he is competent and capable, choosing carefully who to pardon (Aumerle, the Bishop of Carlisle) and who to execute. Problems flood in on him and we end wondering if he is going to be swamped by the sheer volume of the difficulties put in his path – especially if we suspect that Northumberland is too ambitious to remain a loyal counsellor. Finally, Richard's corpse is brought to him. Timothy West speaks of playing this moment:

> The question that you've got to ask yourself is 'How much of a shock is it when you're confronted by Richard's body?' I don't think it's a factual shock, but I do think it's a huge emotional shock to him because this is the moment, really the first moment in the play, when he becomes aware of the appalling responsibilities of kingship which stay with him and begin tq destroy him as a man all through *Henry IV, Part I*. It's interesting that the imagery of growth, of harvest, that has been used so much through the play, is used in this last speech when he says: 'Lords, I protest, my soul is full of woe/That blood should sprinkle me to make me grow' [45–6]. It's a terrible prophecy. It's a reign which is entirely fed by blood. (*Shakespeare Superscribe*, ed. Myra Barrs, [Harmondsworth, 1980], p. 172).

Bolingbroke reveals more of himself in *Henry IV*. He explains how subtly he courted popularity:

> By being seldom seen, I could not stir
> But like a comet I was wond'red at . . .
> And then I stole all courtesy from heaven,
> And dressed myself in such humility
> That I did pluck allegiance from men's hearts
> [*H IV, Pt I*, iii ii 46–7, 50–2]

He also denies aiming at the throne:

> God knows, I had no such intent
> But that necessity so bowed the state
> That I and greatness were compelled to kiss.
> [*H IV, Pt II*, iii i 68–70]

On his deathbed, talking to his son: 'How I came by the crown, O God, forgive!' [*H IV, Pt II*, iv v 218].

York is third in importance among the characters, deliberately made by Shakespeare into a more thoughtful and willing political figure than York actually was. He is first seen sensibly telling Gaunt that rebuking Richard is useless: 'Direct not him whose way himself will choose' [II i 29]. The well-meaning York, Lord Governor in Richard's absence, is overwhelmed by the demands of the job and probably too old for these responsibilities. Meeting the returned Bolingbroke, he denounces 'gross rebellion and detested treason' [II iii 108]. He adopts the easier course, submission to Bolingbroke, then, asked to go to Bristol Castle, shows typical indecision: 'It may be I will go with you, but yet I'll pause;/For I am loath to break our country's laws' [167–8]. In fact, he is at Bristol, silent. This Grand Old Man of the court, a Marshal Pétain, readily accepts the inevitable and invites Bolingbroke to ascend the throne [VI i 111]. In v ii he still laments Richard's fall. Finding his son plotting against the new king, he is suddenly at his most active, begging King Henry to punish the treacherous Aumerle, overeager to prove his loyalty. 'New and sinister motives are in control and there is a large element of panic in York's vehement insistence that Aumerle has earned a traitor's death' (M. M. Reese, *The Cease of Majesty*, [London, 1961], p. 250). In the final scene York is present but does not speak, pushed aside by the rush of events.

York may be viewed in widely differing ways. Swinburne dismissed him as 'an incomparable, an incredible, an unintelligible and a monstrous nullity'. Often he is played for comedy onstage. Struggling to deal with all the problems, most of all Bolingbroke's invasion, he splutters 'Go, fellow, get thee home, provide some carts' [II ii 106], which, writes Reese, is 'a classic in the annals of military helplessness' (Ibid., 248). His 'Come, cousin,/I'll dispose of you' [II ii 116–17] is unintentionally comic: demanding his boots three times in v ii is also absurd. Comic interpretations of York arise more from the lack of other humour in the play than centrally from the character.

Coleridge praised him: 'The admirable character of York. Religious loyalty struggling with a deep grief and indignation at the king's vices and follies; and adherence to his word

once given in spite of all, even the most natural feelings'. He
has been seen as representing England, and as expressing
Christian stoicism and magnanimity as the Elizabethans
understood these (by James A. Riddell, 'The Admirable
Character of York,' *Texas Studies in Literature & Language*, 21,
1979, pp. 492–502). The York of the play is simply vacillating
and elderly, unequal to the tasks and challenges – finally,
perversely, overenergetic to prove his loyalty even at the
expense of his son.

4 'RICHARD II' AS HISTORY PLAY

Critics used to worry about defining the history play, for
example, whether the form was the same as the chronicle
play. Coleridge tried to place the form as between epic and
tragedy. Lily Campbell wrote that 'tragedy deals with an
ethical world; history with a political world' (*Shakespeare's
Histories*, [San Marino, California, 1947], p. 307), that the
subject of tragedy was private relationships and that of
history public life. This distinction does not fit with the texts;
though Richard is accorded little private life, he is clearly
viewed as man as well as king. John Wilders makes a rather
more accurate distinction: 'A tragedy is devoted chiefly to
the struggles of one character, and his death. ... The
impression created by a history play is that the life of a
nation has neither beginning nor ending' (*The Lost Garden*,
[1978], pp. 5–6). Northrop Frye expresses succinctly the way
Shakespeare's histories have both elements: '*Richard II* and
Richard III are tragedies insofar as they resolve on those
defeated kings; they are histories insofar as they resolve on
Bolingbroke and Richmond, and the most one can say is that
they lean toward history' (*Anatomy of Criticism*, [Princeton,
N.J., 1957], p. 284).

In modern times we have readily accepted the form of the
history play. Gordon Daviot's popular 1930s play, *Richard of
Bordeaux*, ends with Richard deposed but still alive (though
from Shakespeare or textbooks we know his fate). Famous

plays like Bernard Shaw's *St. Joan*, T. S. Eliot's *Murder in the Cathedral* and Robert Bolt's *A Man for All Seasons* all end in the execution or killing of a noble main character, though this has not required them to carry the label, 'historical tragedy'.

That some plays are set in the past and show actual figures from that time can be easily accepted. As audience we hold in mind the particular period (shown at least in costume, if not by dirt, cruelty and disease), the historical figures and the story, shaped by a writer toward a moral, a tragic effect or a theatrical experience. The subject may appeal as an escape to a different world, as a study of a remarkable man or woman, or as a think-piece with a message. (Brecht argued that the less the audience could readily recognise on stage, the more their minds were freed for thinking.)

Richard II shows the fall of a king. Watching this, we certainly wonder how far Richard is to be blamed for his defeat and how far sympathised with. What should Richard have done differently? What might we have done differently in Richard's position? Are Richard's advisers to be blamed? And what will Bolingbroke be like as king? Is the change for better or worse? Such questions readily come to mind. The Elizabethans, however, probably more than ourselves, looked to history for lessons. Shakespeare was pointing to issues of monarchy, government and power relevant to his own times. Two facts indicate just how crucial this was in the 1590s, with Queen Elizabeth I in her sixties and without an heir. The Earl of Essex, on the eve of a desperate, futile attempt to overthrow the Queen in 1601, commanded a performance of this play, presumably to show the possibility and desirability of deposing a monarch – Shakespeare and the actors were probably fortunate to escape punishment. Second, although *Richard II* was printed in 1597, the deposition scene was omitted: the content was too subversive at that date. It was first printed in 1608, by which time James I was securely enthroned.

Shakespeare may have intended only to start his audiences asking questions. York states the dilemma clearly, the conflict of two rights:

> Both are my kinsmen.
> T'one is my sovereign, whom both my oath
> And duty bids defend. T'other again
> Is my kinsman, who the King hath wronged,
> Whom conscience and my kindred bids to right. [II ii 111–15]

If deposition was ever justified, was it justified in the case of Richard?

Scholarly discussion has continued for decades on these problems: the pace of scholars' discussions is usually very slow. E. M. W. Tillyard in *Shakespeare's History Plays* in 1944 announced clear views which were generally accepted for a long time. Tillyard saw Shakespeare forming his view of the events of the previous 220 years from some of 'the best educated and most thoughtful writers outside the theatre as well as within' (p. 70), notably the historical chronicles of Edward Hall (1548) and the multi-author moralistic historical poems, *A Mirror for Magistrates* (1555, published 1559). These texts expressed 'the Tudor myth' of a golden age in the long reign of Edward III (1327–77) followed by the inadequacies of Richard II and then nearly a hundred years of disaster attributed to the deposing of Richard. Though Richard admittedly made mistakes, only tyrants and usurpers could be overthrown and Richard's shortcomings did not justify Bolingbroke's seizure of power. That rebellion was almost always wrong was the chief message of Hall, *A Mirror for Magistrates*, and – according to Tillyard – of Shakespeare.

Tillyard went on to argue that Shakespeare planned the sequence of four plays, *Richard II*, the two parts of *Henry IV* and *Henry V*, from the start, though these plays were not in fact written till a few years later. Thus, writes Tillyard, the formal, archaic style of *Richard II* is a *deliberate* contrast to that of *Henry IV*. Bolingbroke's world is kept purposely embryonic and the hints about future discord are carefully placed.

Tillyard based his view of Shakespeare's message not only on Hall and *A Mirror for Magistrates* but on his understanding of how Elizabethans saw their world: he described this as *The Elizabethan World Picture*, his even more influential 1943 study.

The key was order, as set out in Ulysses' speech in *Troilus and Cressida*:

> The heavens themselves, the planets, and this centre
> Observe degree priority and place
> Insisture course proportion season form
> Office and custom, in all line of order.   [I iii 85–8]

Political order on earth mirrored cosmic order. And, Tillyard was able to argue, this doctrine was not often clearly set out in the writings of the time precisely because it was universally accepted – always a difficult proposition to counter. Tillyard, in fact, gave readers history plays which expressed Tudor ideology and the commonplaces of their time.

But would Shakespeare, innovative elsewhere, be 'content to follow the lead of the plodding didacticists who supposedly created the genre of the History Play, and like them dedicate his art to moralistic and propagandistic purposes' (Robert Ornstein, *A Kingdom for a Stage*, p. 2)?

So Ornstein in 1972 returns to the Tudor chroniclers and finds that they all condemn Richard for 'his personal vices and his political rapacity and disregard of law' (Ibid., p. 14). If Shakespeare is defending Richard and denouncing Bolingbroke, he appears to be the one out of step with prevailing opinions of the time. Ornstein also demonstrates that, if Shakespeare were expressing the 'Tudor myth' in his history plays, he does it very badly: the Epilogue to *Henry V* does not mention the original sin against Richard II and the three mentions of Richard in *Henry VI* 'scarcely convince us that it was the cause of Henry VI's calamities' (Ibid., p. 16). Primarily this critic argues for the major point of the play to be personal, not historical–political: Shakespeare 'places as great a value on the sanctity of personal relations in the History Plays as in the tragedies, because he intuits that order depends, not on concepts of hierarchy and degree, but on the fabric of personal and social relationships which is woven by ties of marriage, kinship and friendship, by communal interests, and ideals of loyalty and trust' (p. 222).

Jan Kott, from Poland, in his influential 1960s book *Shakespeare Our Contemporary*, sees a harsh, unchanging, relentless world-view: 'If one wishes to interpret Shakespeare's world as the real world, one should start the reading of the plays with the Histories, and in particular with *Richard II* and *Richard III* ... Shakespeare exposes in them the mechanism of power directly, without resorting to subterfuge or fiction. He de-thrones regal majesty, strips it of all illusion'. Shakespeare's view of history, he asserts, is 'that history has no meaning and stands still, or constantly repeats its cruel cycle' (pp. 3, 49, 37). The only available roles are victor and victim.

Rethinking the attitudes displayed in the history plays starts for John Wilders in his *The Lost Garden* in the conviction that chiefly they are 'brilliantly constructed works for the theatre' (p. 9). Shakespeare has of course a viewpoint on moral and political conduct, that he sees a corrupt – or at least prosaic – world, with a contrasted heroic, inspiring one in the distant past. Mere mortals struggle to make decisions knowing the inevitable imperfection of their judgements; Time and Fortune combine to thwart and limit human achievement. The monarchy may possibly have been glorious before Richard II's reign but this view is bleak and pessimistic about both kings and their subjects, now and in the times depicted in the plays.

That *Richard II* was seen by Shakespeare from the start as the first of a sequence of four history plays has been widely believed. On the other hand, some years elapse before Shakespeare continued writing the supposed quartet and dramatists cannot expect audiences to see four related plays in the correct order. References back to *Richard II* in the later plays may be seen either as providing the context in the broader sweep of English history or as Shakespeare's 'commercials' for his other works, like the reminder of *Julius Caesar* given in *Hamlet*. That *Richard II* is stylistically different from *Henry IV* is more easily explained as Shakespeare trying out a different style than by his deliberately planning a contrast with unwritten texts to follow.

Current opinion leans to seeing Shakespeare as thinking critically and independently about the events he depicts, with his own interpretation – which may or may not coincide with a prevailing Tudor myth of history, which itself may or may not have existed. Shakespeare, in fact, was a critic of ideas, not their mouthpiece. Probably too his view was not a rapid response to the facts in Holinshed but based on wide and thorough reading.

We may legitimately argue – endlessly – about what view of history is expressed in *Richard II* and whether it is distinctively Shakespeare's view, the received opinion of his time or some blend of both. However, there is no need to argue about whether this drama is about historical events or about a man's tragic fall. Clearly, *Richard II* is both and the Tudor doctrine, a legal fiction, of the two bodies of a king enables us readily to keep both facets of the play simultaneously in mind. Edmund Plowden expressed the crown lawyers' belief of the mid-16th century: 'For the king has in him two Bodies, *viz*, a Body natural, and a Body politic'. The former is mortal; the latter abstract, 'consisting of Policy and Government, and constituted for the Direction of the People, and the Management of the public weal . . . What the king does in his Body politic cannot be invalidated or frustrated by any disability in his natural Body'. The two natures are fused at the moment of coronation (J. Barton, *The King's Two Bodies*, [Princeton, N.J., 1957], quoted by Ernest H. Kantorowicz, p. 7). Elizabethans knowing this concept would see the drama's distinction between private life and public face, between good poet and bad king, between the individual and the role he had to play.

If the play is seen as historical fact, or as the Hall/Holinshed/late Elizabethan view of those facts, we may miss the timeless abstract themes. James Winny identifies in Shakespeare's histories man's 'instinctive desire for society and friendship, and for the deeper satisfactions of true allegiance, faithful service, and ordered prerogative' (*The Player King*, p. 29). I would add several other themes: the lust for power, the disenchantment of achievement, the experience of defeat, the conflict between traditional loyalties and realistic adjustment to the winning side, the contrast between high-principled aims and the ruthless realities, the constant choice between punishment and forgiveness, the continued threat from the deposed.

The play is precisely located in different parts of England

and Wales. The lists scene [I iii] is at Coventry, in the
Midlands. Bolingbroke, though coming from Brittany in
France, lands on the north coast and makes the long march
south-west through the Cotswolds to Berkeley and to Bristol.
Richard's return from Ireland is to Barkloughly and he
moves on north-west to Flint, where he is met by Bolingbroke.
The deposition takes place in the presence of parliament in
London, then Richard is sent to the dungeon of Pomfret
(Pontefract) Castle, in Yorkshire. These castles remain, in
ruins, scanty at Pontefract though part of the room in which
Richard was probably held survives, as do fragmentary
battlements at Flint and substantial ruins at Harlech (the
Barkloughly of the play).

Gaunt's famous dying speech makes England the play's
subject (though we should note the irony that he speaks to
York, who does not need this inspirational address, and that
Gaunt manages little more than scolding once Richard has
arrived). Gaunt pictures the potential of England and its
present decline. The Gardeners talk of 'our sea-walled
garden, the whole land' [III iv 43] and how it should be
governed. In *Richard II* the destiny of England is determined
by conflict among the nobility: six dukes (Gaunt; Bolingbroke,
Duke of Hereford; Mowbray, Duke of Norfolk; Aumerle;
York; Surrey), two earls (Northumberland and Salisbury);
four lords (Ross, Willoughby, Berkeley, Fitzwater) and five
knights (Bushy, Green, Bagot, Scroop, Exton). The Commons
are present at the deposition [IV i 271]: they are wealthy
gentry. The emblematic verse-speaking Gardeners may
plausibly be played as monks rather than as eloquent
workers.

The unseen 'common people' are contemptuously dismissed
by Richard as 'slaves' [I iv 24, 27]; York is scornful of them
for the way in which they mocked Richard and welcomed
Bolingbroke as their new king [v ii 11–36]. Richard's
indifference to his subjects finally alters because of his
suffering and in his last moments he responds to the simple
humanity of the Groom [v v 67–97].

5 WHAT DOES THE PLAY MEAN TO US NOW?

Richard II looks as though it should provide evidence on what Shakespeare himself really believed. The current fashion is to see him as conservative, as Graham Greene places him: 'If there is one supreme poet of conservatism, of what we now call the Establishment, it is he' ('The Virtue of Disloyalty', *The Portable Graham Greene*, [Harmondsworth, 1977], p. 606). Colin MacInnes concludes: 'It is hard ... to pinpoint Shakespeare's moral attitudes, unless to say that he respected formal society, disliked cruelty, and seemed to believe evil won its own retribution' (*No Novel Reader*, [London, 1975], p. 18). And Martin Fido: 'When we look at the plays, we find the cautious conservatism of his business dealings and social aspirations confirmed ... From start to finish we find an acceptance of the *status quo*, a respect for the established social order, and a distaste for change ... The truest description we can from our knowledge give of Shakespeare the man is, I believe, an unusually cautious conservative' (*Shakespeare*, [London, 1975], p. 140). *Richard II* perhaps presents what might be called a fatalistic view of human affairs: problems continue, whoever is king. Once Bolingbroke is ruler, like his predecessor, he has to deal with quarrelsome gage-throwing nobles, with Aumerle's plot [v ii, v iii] and then with more rebellions at the start of the last scene. The sense of events endlessly recurring is in fact such that I half-expect at the end the arrival of messengers with news that York is dying and that the Irish are rebelling again.

On the other hand, *Richard II* shows that rebellion is possible, and can succeed (though none of the plots of Shakespeare's lifetime against Elizabeth I had succeeded). *Richard II* might also be said to demystify the remote figure of the monarch, showing not only feet of clay but multiple incompetencies. The play shows us the actuality of a forced handing over of a crown, the legalising of a coup d'état. Further, clearly God and His angels do not rescue the king of England when he is in difficulties. And the true character of many of the Top People is exposed: Bolingbroke comes back to claim what is due to *him*, not to restore those past glories of England which John of Gaunt hymns.

On the political level, the play asks questions. What is a good monarch like? What may morally and legitimately be done by a nation faced with a bad ruler? Will a change of monarch be an improvement? Whether or not *Richard II* is seen as a prologue to *Henry IV*, the change solves few problems. I doubt if we can decide whether or not Shakespeare approved of the deposing of Richard. I find clarity on the level of the individual: Shakespeare can identify readily with the misery of the man deposed.

The specifics of Divine Right are remote to late 20th-century audiences, as is hereditary monarchy to most of the world. It is also difficult to find any equivalent to the position Richard believed himself to have (which was not exactly power, for it crumbled as soon as Bolingbroke dared his challenge). Charles I, Louis XVI, the last Tsar took it for granted that they had absolute authority for life. Drawing this parallel, the 1981 Young Vic production was set in Russia in 1917, with Richard as the Tsar, a complacent monarch who could not see how his world was changing. Nikolas Grace, playing Richard, commented: 'This is a play about how society can unbalance a seat of power, and it doesn't much matter whether that seat of power is Richard Nixon or the Shah. People are interested now in the chemistry of radical politics' (*The Times*, 22 Feb. 1981). Bolingbroke, though, represents himself much more than society or radical politics. As for the emotions of the deposed, the Dalai Lama, god-king of Tibet, deposed, driven into exile by the Chinese invasion in 1959 and still living in India may be the one man today who can understand the astonishment and the misery of the divinely-appointed ruler ruthlessly overthrown.

Ian McKellen tells of the impact of the play in Czechoslovakia:

> In 1969 I played Richard II in a production which we took round England and then briefly to Europe and we went to Czechoslovakia ... We concentrated on the humanity of the characters rather than their political nature. We thought of the political factions as a family, Richard II as a man with cousins

and uncles and other relatives, and I think it was in that sense that we looked at the politics in it. However, we landed in Czechoslovakia only six months after the Prime Minister, Dubcek, had been removed by his neighbouring allies, the Russians. One result of this political change was that they didn't want visiting foreigners with their plays. They tried to stop our visit, but it was too late. ... When I came to the speech where Richard II returns from Ireland to discover that his nation has been overrun by his cousin Bolingbroke, and he kneels down on the earth and asks the stones and the nettles and the insects to help him in his helpless state against the armies who had invaded his land, I could hear something I had never heard before, nor since, which was a whole audience apparently weeping. It shakes me now to think about it, because in that instant I realised that the audience were crying for themselves. They recognised in Richard II their own predicament of only six months previously when their neighbours and as it were their cousins had invaded their land, and all they had were sticks and stones to throw at the tanks.

I would never have talked about the play in those terms.

We hadn't seen it as directly relevant to any modern political situation. Shakespeare couldn't have known about communism, about the East or the West. Afterwards I said to one of the new men, the anti-Dubcek faction, to one of their leaders who was in the audience, 'Who did you side with in the play, Richard II or Bolingbroke? The man on the ground or the invader? And he said, "Both right, both wrong."' (*Playing Shakespeare*, [1984], pp. 191–2, quoted by John Barton.)

Richard II prompted Mark Amory to recall the events in Uganda in 1970: 'It suggests the deposing of Frederick Mutesa, Kabaka of Buganda, 36th of his line, elegant, sophisticated, but careless of his country and, when faced by squat Milton Obote, fatally lacking in troops. The chaos that followed led to Idi Amin . . . The Kabaka died in Bermondsey' (*The Spectator*, 21 Nov. 1981).

The play reminds Samuel Schoenbaum of the fall of President Richard Nixon, forced to resign in 1974 by the threat of impeachment for his involvement in the Watergate burglary: 'The parallels are imprecisely general, except for one haunting detail which escaped nobody. When Richard in the deposition scene has divested himself of crown and sceptre, and with his own tears washed away his balm, 'What more remains?' he asks his tormentors.

Northumberland, implacable, presses on:

> No more but that you read
> These accusations and these grievous crimes
> Committed by your person and your followers
> Against the state and profit of this land,
> That by confessing them the souls of men
> May deem that you are worthily deposed.   [IV i 222–7]

This was, as you will recall, the burning issue after the other deposition. In neither instance was a confession of wrongdoing insisted upon or obtained, although Nixon had his Northumberlands. Nor need I remind you of the consequences for his successor when pardon followed' ('Shakespeare's Histories: the Presence of the Past,' *Shakespeare and Others*, [1985], pp. 101–2).

Finally, in this quest to find an immediacy in these 600-year-old events, the playwright John Arden quotes Richard's speech on the Irish when he sets out to reconquer the island:

> We must supplant those rough rug-headed kerns
> Which live like venom where no venom else
> But only they have privilege to live   [II i 156–8]

Arden comments: 'Not "the Irish are being a nuisance so we have to *subdue* them": but "it is our absolute duty to *supplant* them simply because they exist in their own way in their own country"'. Arden explains: 'In *Richard II* almost everything the King says and does is heavily (and in the end successfully) challenged by someone – Bolingbroke, Gaunt, or whoever. His Irish wars alone escape criticism, except in so far as they are criminally funded and ineptly timed. In fact, they are seen to be one of his few attempts to behave like the proper English King so desired by John of Gaunt to redeem the country from degradation: "England, that was wont to conquer others,/Hath made a shameful conquest of itself" [II i 65–6].' So, Arden argues, Shakespeare has contributed to an attitude of mind which continues to support the English presence in Ireland. Arden even audaciously supplies the lines which Shakespeare should have written to challenge Richard's attitude, giving these to York:

> Nay, nay, my lord, rug-headed Irish kerns
> Spit no more venom than our English sea-dogs do
> Who bravely strive for liberty of this isle
> 'Gainst Frenchmen or the pirate wolves of Spain.
> Therefore disturb them not; they'll prove good friends
> Once left in calm enjoyment of their own.
> ('Rug-headed Irish Kerns and British Poets', *New Statesman*, 13 July 1979, p. 56, and 'Shakespeare: Guilty', *New Statesman*, 10 Aug. 1979, p. 199).

Approaching from a different tack, we may ask what is the present-day appeal of a piece about a man who wallows in self-pity. Harold Hobson in 1947 accounted thus for the appeal of the play in our time: 'Self-pity; lamentation; hysteria. We come closer to the secret of *Richard II*'s popularity in such considerations as these. We have lost the robust confidence of the nineteenth century. The world to-day darts hither and thither directionless. It grieves over the hardness of its fate, just as Richard did. Of all Shakespeare's kings, he is its prime spokesman. And, if not with spirit, if not with courage, he speaks beautifully, with words that twine about the heart. Let us not be too hard upon him, though. But we might well be harder upon ourselves' (*Theatre*, 1948, p. 141).

A Canadian critic finds an approach to the drama that avoids issues of power and authority. Gina Mallett writes: 'The only way to go to most of Shakespeare's history plays is to go with the firm understanding that you're going to see the British Wild West, a great mythic landscape peopled with outsized folk, heroes, rascals, double-dealers, politicians, and not surprisingly, very few women' (*Toronto Star*, 7 June 1979, C3). This emphasises the naked struggles, the uncomplicated emotions and the sense of rival *groups*, rather than individuals.

48

PART TWO: PERFORMANCE

6 INTRODUCTION

Richard II has grown in popularity and reputation in the 20th
century. Productions in this century have taken place under
two shadows. C. E. Montague, in an eloquent 1899 review of
Frank Benson in the title-role, defined Richard as good poet
and bad king: 'The capable and faithful artist in the same
skin as the incapable and unfaithful king ... Shakespere
meant to draw in Richard not only a rake and muff on a
throne and falling off it but, in the same person, an exquisite
poet: to show with one hand how kingdoms are lost and with
the other how the creative imagination goes about its work;
to fill the same man with the attributes of a feckless wastrel
in high place and with the quite distinct but not incompatible
attributes of a typical, a consummate artist' (*Richard II: A
Casebook*, p. 64). So 'most Richards today, taking a tip from
C. E. Montague on Benson, aim at a positively Proustian
portrait of self-awareness', wrote Philip Hope-Wallace as late
as 1952 (*Manchester Guardian*, 30 Dec. 1952). Yet Montague's
view is indebted as much to Walter Pater, writing on
'Shakespeare's English Kings' in 1889, as he is to Frank
Benson's performance, critic and actor equally shaping
Montague's judgement.

The second shadow was of Sir John Gielgud and his
beautiful voice, first heard in the part at the Old Vic in 1929
and again at the Queen's in 1937. Gielgud focused on superb
delivery of verse, perhaps emphasising Richard as pathetic,
and certainly a man unfitted for the demanding duties of a
ruler. Gielgud himself has written well about the role:
'Richard is one of the rare parts in which the actor may
indulge himself, luxuriating in the language he has to speak,
and attitudinizing in consciously graceful poses'. The actor
'must somehow contrive at the same time to execute the
poetic intricacies of the text with a full appreciation of its

The 1973 R.S.C. production directed by John Barton.

1. 'Swear by the duty that you owe to God', (I iii 180) centre group standing: York (Sebastian Shaw), Richard (Richard Pasco), Gaunt (Tony Church); kneeling: Mowbray (Denis Holmes), Bolingbroke (Ian Richardson).
Photograph © T. Holte Picture Library

2. 'See, see, King Richard doth himself appear', (III iii 62) on the walls of Flint Castle, Richard (Ian Richardson) with Aumerle (Nickolas Grace).
Photograph © T. Holte Picture Library.

The 1973 R.S.C. production directed by John Barton.

3. Richard (Richard Pasco) returns from Ireland.
Photograph © T. Holte Picture Library

4. The deposition (IV i). Bolingbroke (Richard Pasco) holds the crown with Richard (Ian Richardson).
Photograph © T. Holte Picture Library

5. 'For there it is, cracked in a hundred shivers', (IV i 288), in the 1980 R.S.C. production directed by Terry Hands with Richard (Alan Howard), Bolingbroke (David Suchet), Abbot of Westminster (Paul Webster) and York (Tony Church).
Photograph © T. Holte Picture Library

6. The 1982 Théâtre du Soleil production (III iv) directed by Ariane Mnouchkine. The Queen (right), her maid and two gardeners. Photograph © Théâtre du Soleil, Paris.

musical intention . . . Unfortunately, throughout the tragedy, the verse seems to be too evenly distributed, and often with more music than sense of character . . . The great problem, as in all Shakespearian plays, is to achieve a straightforward musical rendering of the verse, and yet to combine this with a sense of exciting actuality in the action' (*Richard II: A Casebook*, pp. 77–80). Derek Jacobi, preparing to play the part on television, found the same problem with the verse, expressing it in these terms: 'Every line in it is amazingly beautiful. You can't go through the entire play saying "Oh gosh, this is beautiful, isn't it? Oh, this is wonderful stuff." It is, but you've really got to avoid that and forget it' (BBC TV edn, p. 25).

Thus actors playing Richard have attempted to find ways to play him other than as poet-unfitted-to-be-king and to do justice to the verse but not at the expense of the human being speaking the lines. Alec Guinness, for the Old Vic in 1947, tried for a 'sad neurotic . . . seething and sorrowful at his own impotence'. Guinness caught a 'weary springtime king' (Kenneth Tynan, *A View of the English Stage*, p. 62).

Michael Redgrave at Stratford in 1951 found new insights into Richard. Sir Laurence Olivier identified the key: this was Richard 'as an out-and-out pussy queer, with mincing gestures to match' (*Astonish Us in the Morning*, ed. Alfred Rossi, [London, 1977], p. 97). Richard Findlater put the overt homosexuality in context: 'Instead of Gielgud's kindly, lyrical victim, Redgrave presented a harsh, unsentimentalized portrait, sharp with cruelty, spite and envy; yet the feline homosexual of the early scenes was, for all his malicious weakness, a right royal Plantagenet' (*The Player Kings*, [New York, 1971], p. 252).

The text contains only three lines to suggest Richard is homosexual. Bolingbroke's accusation of Bushy and Green includes:

> You have in manner with your sinful hours
> Made a divorce betwixt his Queen and him,
> Broke the possession of a royal bed [III i 11–13]

Richard is seen with young male favourites. That his court is decadent, extravagant and devoted to pleasure is part of the charge against him. He is choosing friends unwisely, bringing new people to his court rather than the old nobility. Richard's love for the Queen, however, at their farewell [v i] is touching and sincere, so that presenting explicit homosexuality looks like directors desperately seeking the new for its own sake.

Richard David carefully describes Redgrave's appearance: 'His make-up followed the traditional portraits, but with every outline softened and blurred. The fine golden fur of beard dissolved the line of the chin; the hollows and shadows of cheek and brow were toned down into dimples and colourless uniformity. This was a face of putty, a watery face over which the fleeting expressions chased each other – the most constant being an uncertain smile, half self-approving, half placatory, that appeared whenever smiles were least in season. The indecision of the face was reflected in the nervous gestures, the handkerchief picked at and flaunted, the self-conscious jauntiness of gait intended as a sign of assurance but revealing an acute lack of confidence. As a portrait of a wayward weakling, it was superb; but it lacked a quality essential to Shakespeare's Richard – kingliness' ('Shakespeare's History Plays – Epic or Drama?', *Shakespeare Survey*, 6, 1953, p. 134).

Hobson, on the other hand, saw an exceptional quality of strength in this Richard: 'His was the only Richard Britain had seen who could conceivably have suppressed Wat Tyler's rebellion ... Gielgud had offered us a Richard who would have met the rebellion with adolescent tears, Guinness a Richard who would have met it with adolescent verses. Neither of them would conceivably have been able to defeat it. But Redgrave's Richard, on the other hand, would have met and overcome it with strong adolescent nerves'. Redgrave communicated the man's struggles physically, 'the twitching fingers ... the restless movements, the sudden shifting of the eye revealed at what tremendous cost of inner tension the magnificence was kept up' (Hobson, *Theatre in Britain: A Personal View*, [Oxford, 1984], p. 172).

Paul Scofield essayed the part in 1953 at the Lyric, Hammersmith, literally in the shadow of Gielgud, who

directed him. Scofield's Richard was sour, dour, depressed.
Ivor Brown wrote: 'The king was a figure abstract and
remote. Scofield touches the mind more closely than the
feelings. I could not become excited by the fall of this
monarch, who is a chilly, almost prim-looking figure from
the start when capricious debauchery is the temper set down
in the text. Where is the "rash, fierce blaze of riot" that piled
up the bills and made the taxpayers so ready for revolt?' (*The
Observer*, 4 Jan. 1953).

All these productions emphasise Richard as star, a lonely
figure of tragedy. Yet this is a history play and drama is
about conflict. So a new emphasis has been to develop
Bolingbroke as antagonist, a rival, and also a character who
changes during the events of the drama. Further, when
Richard II is seen as the first of a sequence of plays,
Bolingbroke becomes a preliminary to the part which will be
central in the two *Henry IV* plays which follow – as they did
at Stratford in 1951. Then the play is the rise of Bolingbroke.

T. C. Worsley states that in the deposition scene, 'we are
conscious throughout Richard's eloquent dramatics of
Bolingbroke *growing* there on the throne, as, without speaking,
his eyes follow the deposed king's every action . . . For the
special purposes of this production Northumberland and
especially Bolingbroke – subsidiary roles ordinarily speaking –
have to be kept, and are kept, in the centre of the picture'. At
the end Bolingbroke is 'lonely and noble' (*Shakespeare's
Histories at Stratford*, pp. 42–3). For Worsley in 1951
Bolingbroke was still necessarily and definitely a subsidiary
role; later directors and actors have questioned this.

Joan Littlewood, directing the play at Theatre Workshop
in 1954 and 1955, at a time when the Workshop was not
famous but may have been at its best, made Bolingbroke 'the
typical Marxist hero, the revolutionary who overthrows a
regime' and presented the most unattractive Richard ever
seen, 'a weak, treacherous, decadent pervert', Harry Corbett.
The excitement was in 'the relish with which the rebel faction
hunted down their whimpering prey' (Norman Marshall, *The
Producer & the Play*, revised edn, [London, 1962], pp. 299–
300). Howard Goorney of the Workshop comments that 'in
John Bury's stark setting, conceived to emphasise fear and

oppression, we aimed to bring out the hatred and cruelty of
the period . . . Our concern always was for the inner action
behind the lines – what they meant, rather than the poetry'
(*The Theatre Workshop Story*, [London, 1981], p. 101).

Simultaneously in 1955 John Neville played Richard II at
the Old Vic, bringing out his relations to his courtiers: 'We
started out from the point of view that at the beginning of the
play Richard is a playboy king. So a great deal of that part of
the play was taken up with one's attitude to the court, one's
relationship with what are known as "the caterpillars of the
Commonwealth", as they're called in the play. One had a
very close relationship with these young men. They were
young bloods, amusing and witty company' (*Acting in the
Sixties*, ed. Hal Burton, [BBC, London, 1970], p. 101). This
close relationship was shown in performance by Richard
stopping the duel in the third scene on the whispered advice
of Bushy, followed by Richard turning his back to chat to his
friends as Mowbray and Bolingbroke talk [ɪ iii 192–207].

Two major interests in performance, then, are the nature
of Richard (or, more accurately, what facets of Richard's
character are to be emphasised) and the weight to be given
to the rest of the cast. A third issue is whether to play up the
ritual and formality of the big court scenes or to minimise
these and attempt to find more humanity instead. A lesser
problem is that of historical accuracy, whether costumes are
painstakingly correct to the late 14th century and whether
decor is used to transport us into a medieval world.

Ian McKellen first established his name as Richard
(alternating with the lead in Marlowe's *Edward II*) with the
Prospect Company, touring 1968–70, playing in London and
at the Edinburgh Festival, directed by Richard Cottrell.
Ronald Bryden identified what was for McKellen Richard's
tragic flaw, 'the trouble with Richard is royalty. Lapped
from childhood in total obedience, insulated from reality by
instant performance of his slightest will, he is living a fantasy.
Eyes glazed with egoism, voice floating high and remote out
of the gay circle of courtiers ringing him like bright, empty-
headed marigolds, he is a singing gold doll, gloves raised in a
marvellous gesture at once saintly, complacent and hopeless'
(*The Observer*, 17 Nov. 1968). Richard at the start is totally

immersed in the way of life at court, with himself at the head. 'I have seen Richards who have begun with their left leg idly hooked over the throne as if they were in their own backyard: McKellen, however, makes it instantly clear that Richard is steeped in ceremony and that through the years he has come to accept it as proof of his physical inviolability' (Michael Billington, *The Modern Actor*, [London, 1973], p. 78). Starting from this acceptance of the role of monarch, this Richard learns: 'There is comparatively little here of Montague's artist-king, tipsy with grief. Rather, this Richard is a man engaged in the process of discovering his own vulnerability' (Ibid., pp. 78–9). McKellen emphasised particular phrases and lines, as Billington shows:

'I live with bread like you, feel want, taste grief,/*Need friends*'
[III ii 175–6]

These last two words become a cry of anguish, the vowels stretched out to breaking point like pieces of elastic and all the world's pain and desolation suddenly seeming to be compressed into a few seconds. . . .
For well we know, no hand of blood or stone
Can grip the sacred handle of our sceptre
Unless he do profane, steal or usurp. [III iii 79–81]

In the last line his voice soars to a high-pitched scream on *usurp*: a word with sacrilegious connotations for a Plantagenet. For a moment he cannot go on; tears start to drown his words; and he recovers himself only with the boast that 'God omnipotent,/Is mustering in his clouds on our behalf/Armies of pestilence' [85–7]. Compare Gielgud's treatment of the same passage. He ignores the terror behind particular words like 'usurp'. He begins with a breathless, stricken 'We are amazed' and gradually increases volume and tempo until he comes to the 'armies of pestilence; and they shall *strike*/Your children yet unborn'. Having thus established himself at base camp, as it were, he goes on to assault the summit of the speech with its threat of civil war and its terrifying image of lush pastures bedewed with faithful English blood [79–80].

Though Timothy West as Bolingbroke had the basic quality of practicality, McKellen came close to making the role once again a solo turn.

The National Theatre's production, directed by David William in 1972, was judged dull but Ronald Pickup found new, if unrewarding, facets as Richard. 'He begins with dangerous calmness, the tranquillity which often cloaks potential violence. And sure enough a vein of sudden physicality soon emerges, a table over-turned in a flash of temper, an irksome document knocked brutally from the hand of an unsuspecting favourite. The result is that for once in the role it comes as no shock when in the death-scene this self-defeating egoist reveals himself as an accomplished killer. Pickup's is an intensely original reading, owing little to previous performers, though with perhaps a visual hint of the young Gielgud in its moments of languid frailty; this Richard is a coldly regal man, not easily moved and, sadly, just that bit too unmoving' (Frank Cox, *Plays and Players*, May 1972, p. 45). Pickup had found a Richard who was a plausible human being; unfortunately, though, this Richard was not only unmoving, he was fatally uninteresting.

The *Richard* in the BBC television series of all Shakespeare's plays appeared in 1978, one of the first group of six. (The first television *Richard* was in the United States in 1954 with Maurice Evans: it was the most popular Shakespeare on US TV because the audience did not know how the story would end! A scene was written in of Bolingbroke paying Exton to kill the ex-king.) Cedric Messina, the producer, saw that the TV plan made possible the tetralogy: 'These histories are a sort of Curse of the House of Atreus in England' (yet Percy and Northumberland were played by different actors in the later plays!). David Giles directed Derek Jacobi in the title role. The key to Jacobi's approach was, for Clive James, 'Richard had let his divinity run away with him'. He 'was faced with a hard task in transferring the focus from the physique to the mentality. He did it, though'. James admired Jon Finch as Bolingbroke: 'He must play the role on two levels, speaking what is set down for him and transmitting his ambitions – if it is supposed that they exist – by other means. Even when he was standing still you could tell he was heading for the throne of England by the direct route' (*The Crystal Bucket*, [Picador, 1981], pp. 158–9).

A studio set was used and the designer, Tony Abbott,

explained 'What was wanted for *Richard* was an impression of big Gothic medieval architecture. I created units based on Gothic elements and by redressing those units I was able to create Windsor Castle, Pomfret Castle. I went to see Westminster Hall and saw the hammer beams and I looked at Windsor Castle, but what you are trying to create is an environment rather than a specific place: as long as you give an impression in the background that this is Westminster Hall, that is all that is needed' (BBC TV edn, p. 20). Nancy Banks-Smith scorned the unashamed use of a studio: 'England, I die pronouncing it, is now made up of props and flats and painted crowds and the sound of the sea off' (*Guardian Weekly*, 24 Dec. 1978).

Close-ups and cuts between faces in fact underlined scenes effectively. In III i, for example: 'We get all three perspectives: (1) Bolingbroke's righteous indignation at being stripped of his lands and title, his straight-faced lies, and his casual indifference to the beheadings; (2) York's silent protests as Bolingbroke accuses the prisoners of causing not only the rift between Richard and the Queen but that between Richard and Bolingbroke, and his shock at the sound of the beheadings off-frame as Bolingbroke calmly instructs him to send "fair entreaties" and "kind commends" (38); and (3) Bushy and Green's vulnerability, their shirts and bare chests contrasting with the armor of their captors, and their Richard-like impotence as they insult Bolingbroke before being taken away' (Jack Jorgens, 'The BBC-TV Shakespeare Series', *Shakespeare Quarterly*, 30, Summer 1979, p. 414). Giles described how the flexibility of the camera enhanced Richard's soliloquy in prison [v v]: 'It's all about time passing and by using mixes during the speech I think we move it on in time. I don't think we've broken the rhythm: each section of the soliloquy has him in a slightly different place doing something else, so time passes and we just swing the mixes through. It pushes you through a long period of time' (BBC TV edn, p. 23).

Commentators gave moderate praise to the television *Richard*, grudgingly observing that it was rather better than others of the first six.

Brian Bedford played an original and dominant Richard at

Stratford, Ontario, in 1983, directed by Richard Cottrell. He
'indulged himself in regal ceremony, touching the emblems
of monarch (orb, sceptre, sword) as if they were divine
instruments of power . . . Bedford turned the play into a
tragedy of wit in the sense of both irony and cognition. From
the start he was in command: gently mocking about
Bolingbroke's rough manner of speech; simulating dim
forgetfulness about Bolingbroke's genealogical relationship to
him; relishing the panoply of pomp and ceremony at court
. . . With sophistry as his great intellectual weapon, he tried
to find solace in its cutting wit . . . Even in his most abject
misery, this Richard managed to retrieve his satirical,
sardonic wit' (Keith Garebian, 'The 1983 Stratford Festival',
Journal of Canadian Studies, 18, Fall 1983, p. 152). Robert
Cushman saw just how far Bedford's interpretation went:
'Most Richard's play for irony, but Mr. Bedford's was the
completest tease I have seen. Having sent the whole of
England up rotten, he turned on himself; "for God's sake let
us sit upon the ground" (III ii 155) was a self-conscious
bright idea. How much was Richard having fun, and how
much the actor, was difficult to say' (*The Observer*, 14 Aug.
1983). Design brought out the sun, the rose, the garden – the
gardeners' straw hats were shaped like solar discs with rays –
and at the end Bolingbroke, beside Richard's corpse, was
bathed in a red light from a bloody rose.

The productions of *Richard II* examined here are:

1. by the Royal Shakespeare Company, 1973–74, directed
by John Barton, in which Richard Pasco and Ian Richardson
alternated as Richard and Bolingbroke – for the first time
giving equal weight to the latter part.

2. by the Stratford Festival, Ontario, Canada, in 1979,
when three different actors played Richard.

3. by the Royal Shakespeare Company in 1980–81, with
Alan Howard as Richard, directed by Terry Hands.

4. by the Théâtre du Soleil of Vincennes, France, in 1982–
84, directed by Ariane Mnouchkine.

7 ROYAL SHAKESPEARE COMPANY, RICHARD PASCO AND
   IAN RICHARDSON, DIRECTED JOHN BARTON, 1973–74

John Barton's production for the Royal Shakespeare Company
in 1973 was eagerly awaited as he was the most audacious,
as well as the most intellectual, of the company's directors.
RSC programmes, with several pages of quotations, may
provide clues to the director's point of view; more significant,
they are the only way in which the production guides its
audience to a current perspective on the 1595 view of the late
1390s. This programme had two pages by Anne Barton
expounding the doctrine of the king's two bodies, adding
that Shakespeare 'seized upon and explored the latent parallel
between the King and that other two-natured human being,
the Actor'. Nine other quotations are headed, cautiously,
'Sightlines', three of which add to the concept of the king as
simultaneously human and divine, and a fourth offering
Richard as an actor 'prone to the weakness of self-
dramatisation'. (Looking ahead to the RSC's programme for
its 1980 production, six of these excerpts are repeated, but
three passages from Holinshed, Sir Walter Raleigh and *A
Mirror for Magistrates* are added; from the last: 'Whosoever
rebels against any ruler, either good or bad, rebels against
God, and shall be sure of a wretched end'. The three newly-
added sections by modern critics draw out Tudor political
beliefs, as in Brents Stirling: 'Doctrine, plot, and
characterization unfold integrally. With our debts to the
English and American revolutions we cannot admire the
doctrine'. The 1979 Stratford, Ontario, programme stays
with sources, Holinshed and Froissart.)
    Barton in 1973 made substantial changes to the text,
including cutting about 500 lines and adding 50. The changes
can be categorised:
    a) The text was clarified and tidied by eliminating the
minor and forgettable figures of Berkeley (seen only in II iii)
and Scroop (see only in III ii and III iii, in which he does not
speak). Barton substantially rewrote the opening of IV i, to
counter the unintentional comedy of the throwing down of

gages, ending it with Aumerle's 'Who sets me else?' [57], which was moved to line 83.

b) A number of speeches were presented with actors alternating lines of a speech. Bushy's speech, 'Each substance of a grief hath twenty shadows' [ii ii 14] was shared with Green. The Welsh Captain's speech in ii iv 7–17 had each line delivered by one of eight men, standing in line backs to the audience, with music playing on horns. In iii iv the Gardener's lines were divided almost equally between the three gardeners. One intent of these changes was to provide a kind of prophetic Chorus, foreseeing the inevitable fate of Richard; more obviously, such moments were unrealistic and reminded the audience that this was a *theatrical* experience.

c) The Queen's part was slightly increased by assigning her, at iii ii 21, Bushy's lines from ii ii: beginning 'For sorrow's eye, glazed with blinding tears./Divides one thing entire to many objects' [16–23]. This served as a kind of prayer, increasing sympathy for the Queen.

d) Exton, not found in the text till the last three scenes, is seen earlier, delivering Green's lines about Bolingbroke's rebellion, ii ii 49–51, and Scroop's lines in iii ii. This revised Exton has been close to Richard, increasing his villainy as Richard's murderer.

e) Northumberland's role as hard man and No. 2 to the new king is increased by his having Percy's lines in the last scene, in which the Bishop of Carlisle is led out for sentence.

f) The character of Bolingbroke is altered, making him clearly ambitious at the moment of his banishment in i iii. One ambiguous line is added at the end of his last speech: 'Now must I serve a long apprenticehood' (to the kingship?). This changes the position and the implication of what Shakespeare gives him 40 lines earlier, 'Must I not serve a long apprenticehood/To foreign passages' [271–2]. In iii i Bolingbroke's account of the crimes of Bushy and Green, which justify their execution [8–27], is read from a paper, distancing Bolingbroke himself from the sentence. That Bolingbroke is soon weighed down by the responsibilities of kingship is shown by giving him a soliloquy at the start of v iii made up of lines spoken in fact in *2 Henry IV* and previously by Richard [v i 55–9], ending 'Uneasy lies the head that wears the crown!' These lines show the new king sleepless with anxiety, aware of Northumberland's role and afraid of civil war. Stanley Wells explains the effects of these changes: 'The manipulation of Bolingbroke's role, and the additions to it, were clearly designed to increase sympathy for him, to suggest in him an awareness of a cyclical element in human history, and to bring him closer to Richard' (*Royal Shakespeare*, Manchester U.P., 1977, p. 79).

Some of the many striking features of this celebrated production should be itemised.

a) The set, stark and mechanised, was described by Timothy O'Brien, who designed it with Tazeena Firth: 'Picture two walls, set at right angles to the front of the stage, parallel to one another 8 m. apart, 8 m. long, 8 m. high at the upstage ends', sloping steeply towards the audience. 'These triangular walls were 80 cm. thick and had a staircase built into their steep incline with a closed string to either side of the steps, much like the walls of the great sun clocks in Jai Singh's observatory in Jaipur. Next a bridge was designed to span from one wall to the other . . . It was possible to raise and lower the bridge on the slope of the walls. When the bridge was high, it was far away and lost amongst the borders of the stage; when it was low, it reached the stage close to the audience'. The narrow staircases, suggesting ascent and descent as the key to the drama, are shown in Plate 1. O'Brien continues: 'The form of the walls was suggestive enough of "the sea-walled garden", of a court in a Christian country, or of castles not to need an imitated surface of stone, but instead it seemed better to dress them in the same dark cork as covered the theatre's forestage walls, and to set the walls on the deep brown carpet provided as stage covering for the season' ('Designing a Shakespeare Play: *Richard II*,' *Deutsche Shakespeare-Gesellschaft West Jahrbuch*, 1974, [Heidelberg], pp. 114, 116).

The bridge, partly raised, gave Richard a platform on which to preside at the lists and a conspicuous place to die. Memorably, the bridge slowly descended at Flint Castle when Richard said 'Down, down I come' [III iii 178].

b) A little pot of earth stood downstage. Bolingbroke touched it as he left: 'Then, England's ground, farewell! Sweet soil, adieu' [I iii 306]. Richard fingered it on his return from Ireland: 'Dear earth, I do salute thee with my hand' [III ii 6] and the Gardener put a sprig into it as he announced 'Here in this place/I'll set a bank of rue' [III iv 104–5]. The Bishop of Carlisle touched it referring to 'this cursed earth' [IV i 147], as did the Queen for 'rebellious earth' [v i 5].

The programme quotes from a 1947 article by Richard Altick: '"Earth", while it emblematizes the foundation of kingly pride and power, is also a familiar symbol of the vanity of human life and of what, in the Middle Ages, was an illustration of that vanity – the fall of kings' ('Symphonic Imagery in *Richard II*', *Richard II: A Casebook*, pp. 101–30). The plot of soil also stresses the play's concern with the destiny of the whole land, England.

c) The opening dumbshow: 'Before the house lights dimmed there appeared a figure resembling Shakespeare, carrying a book resembling the First Folio.' He looked at a scarecrow with royal robes, crown and mask, 'opened the book, and signalled for the appearance of the actors. They filed on in two columns, one headed by Ian Richardson, the other by Richard Pasco. They all wore rehearsal costume. The leaders of the company joined Shakespeare at the dais, each holding one side of the book. Shakespeare mounted the pyramid, took the crown and the mask from the scarecrow, and placed them on the open book. The two actors held crown and mask high between them [anticipating the deposition scene]; Shakespeare bowed to the actor who was to play Richard at that performance, and gradually the actors took on their costumes and wigs, in view of the audience, assuming the appearance of the characters they were to play. The robing of Richard was a kind of coronation ritual; the court knelt to him, chanting words not in the text: "God save the King! Long live the King! May the King live forever!" Richard faced the audience, echoed "May the King live forever!" and removed his mask. Thus the director prefigured the play's concern with the inevitable tension between the demands made by the office of kingship, of being God's deputy on earth, and the capacities of the human being who has to try to fill a role that is inevitably too big for him. And, even more important to this production, he associated this with the idea of the actor assuming the role that he had to play on stage' (Stanley Wells, pp. 75–6).

d) In I ii the Duchess of Gloucester was played as a ghost, emerging from a grave carrying a skull, with echo effects for her lines. Her call for revenge suggests perhaps the Ghost in *Hamlet*, also requiring vengeance for a murder, and the convention of revenge plays.

e) In I iii, at the lists at Coventry, Mowbray and Bolingbroke were on hobbyhorses, in costumes making the actors appear to be riding on horses (as had been done in the Paris and London performances of Jean Anouilh's *Becket*). This was the first of several effective uses of variously-stylised horses. At the start of II iii Northumberland is on a black horse, with Bolingbroke walking beside him, dressed as a monk (one of many monks in black, brown and white robes in the play) chanting 'Kyrie Eleison'. Ross and Willoughby are on black horses when they join them, supported by the text, 'bloody with spurring, fiery red with haste' [58].

Richard is on a white horse when he returns from Ireland in III ii (Plate 2). He dismounts to salute his land, remounts when Aumerle urges 'Remember who you are' [83] but dismounts again, noisily dropping his sword, when told that Bushy, Green and the Earl of Wiltshire have been beheaded [144].

f) Mirrors, in fact of clear glass, are used three times, not only where required by the text in the deposition scene. First, at I iv 42: 'A mirror is handed to Richard II by his courtiers who are discussing the prospects for the upcoming Irish Wars. During the matinee at Stratford-upon-Avon Richard Pasco's light-headed skipping king remained uninterested in the military planning until, quite suddenly, he donned a bright plumed helmet and was able to gaze admiringly at his brilliant reflection in the mirror. He was now obviously delighted at the thought of leading his troops into battle. During the same scene at the evening performance Ian Richardson provided a sharp contrast to Pasco's narcissism and sense of self-love. There was more than a hint of impish cynicism and distaste on Richardson's features as he cast a look at himself in the mirror which had delighted Pasco. This Richard seemed to despise his own reflection'. When Richard smashes the mirror in IV i at line 287, Pasco drops it 'with reluctance as a gesture of defeated self-pity' while Richardson throws it down 'with a definite sign of relief calling a halt to the role he has been playing in life and which he has perhaps secretly resented' (Peter Ansorge, *Plays and Players*, June 1973, p. 39). Bolingbroke's comment, 'The shadow of your sorrow hath destroyed/The shadow of your face' [291–2] in this performance was repeated by all the attendant lords speaking together. Bolingbroke slowly put the broken frame of the mirror over Richard's neck, so that in turn it suggested a halo, a crown and a noose. Richard wears the broken frame, a bizarre chain of office, in his last two scenes, v i and v v, taking it and looking through it at the groom, who is Bolingbroke.

g) At Flint Castle [III iii] Richard wears a splendid golden robe, suggesting the sun and eagle's wings, and he spreads his arms immediately before his descent to submit (Plate 3).

h) The power and influence of Northumberland in the later part of the drama is shown visually by his acting on stilts, a strange effect echoed by Anthony Sher's famous Richard III of 1984–85, leaning forward on to crutches. Northumberland has become a bird, with beak and claws, as he towers above Richard's farewell to his Queen in v i. This bird presumably derives from the several birds mentioned – falcon, eagle, pelican, owl and lark.

i) v ii begins with the York family and their attendants, wrapped against the cold, playing children's games and singing Christmas carols. A snowman melted as York described Richard and Bolingbroke entering London, suggested by Richard's lament after the deposition:

> O that I were a mockery king of snow,
> Standing before the sun of Bolingbroke,
> To melt myself away in water-drops!   [IV i 259–61]

When York said 'To Bolingbroke are we sworn subjects now' [v ii 39], winter clothes were discarded and spring colours seen.

j) The groom who visits Richard in prison in v v is a

hooded figure with a rustic accent. He brings a toy horse, which he hands over as he speaks:

> When Bolingbroke rode on roan Barbary,
> That horse that thou so often hast bestrid,
> That horse that I so carefully have dressed!   [v v 78–80]

When Richard lamented 'Yet I bear a burden like an ass,/Spurred, galled, and tired by jauncing Bolingbroke' [93–94], he suddenly recognises the groom as Bolingbroke, who throws back his hood. 'Richard took from his own neck the frame of the mirror and held it between them, so that each saw the other as if he were a reflection of himself . . . They knelt for a moment in this pose before Bolingbroke left on the line: "What my tongue dares not, that my heart shall say"' [97]. Wells interprets this as a 'recognition on Bolingbroke's part that both he and Richard have been the playthings of fortune, both finally united in a Wilfred Owen-like "strange meeting" in which their shared experience of the hollowness of the kingly crown draws them together more powerfully than their former rivalry sets them apart. Here we saw them as themselves, neither needing to act a part' (p. 79). The moment remains puzzling: is Bolingbroke as the visitor to be taken literally? This is like dramatists who will write meetings of Queen Elizabeth and Mary, Queen of Scots, because it *should* have happened. Judith Cook explains the director's intention: 'It is an image which is given dramatic form. Richard, as the divinely appointed King, is trapped in his role, and inhibited by it from true contact with other, merely mortal, men. Only when in prison, uncrowned, can he speak simply as a man. Bolingbroke too, as soon as he becomes King, is trapped, but he, unlike Richard, was not groomed for kingship, and therefore feels the weight of the restrictions the crown imposes on him very early in his reign. This realization of the role-playing his position demands, and his inner sympathy with Richard, finds an expressionistic, if not realistic, outlet in his visit to the prison. The King is there, naked of his role, dressed in a prison garment; Bolingbroke as the groom can confront him similarly naked. Thus stripped the two men are enabled to say those things which in the outside political world were disallowable' (*Directors' Theatre*, [London, 1974], p. 12).

k) Richard before death is hoisted four metres into the air by his wrists, then shot in the back by Exton with a gilded crossbow. Richard thus soars into the heavens at the moment of death and at this height recalls his last moment of looking triumphant on the walls of Flint Castle.

l) The end: 'Coronation music returned, and the figure of Shakespeare, seen at the beginning of the play, appeared as if to crown Bolingbroke, who turned towards him, his back to the audience. Drums rolled powerfully in crescendo. Courtiers gathered around Bolingbroke. He was invested with the golden robe of kingship. All but two of his courtiers fell away, the music reached a climax, and the king turned to us. The drums suddenly ceased, and the courtiers beside Bolingbroke threw back their hoods and revealed themselves, one as the actor who had been playing Richard, the other as the actor who had been playing Bolingbroke' (Wells, p. 80). The glittering robe between them was topped by a skull.

This powerful image must refer back to Richard's lament

> For within the hollow crown
> That rounds the mortal temples of a king
> Keeps death his court; and there the antic sits,
> Scoffing his state and grinning at his pomp   [III ii 160–3]

We should think too of the quotation in the programme from Eugene Ionesco: 'When Richard II dies, it is really the death of all I hold most dear that I am watching; it is I who die with Richard II'.

All these effects can be justified from the text. Some critics felt they underlined unnecessarily, but only Northumberland as fearsome giant bird and the melting snowman risk distracting from the words. Many of them were modified, largely for practical staging reasons, when the play went to the Aldwych Theatre in London the following year.

That Richard Pasco and Ian Richardson alternated in the roles of Richard and Bolingbroke gave – for the first time – virtually equal weight to the part of Bolingbroke. Barton saw the two men as alike, as Richard's buckets speech suggests:

Now is this golden crown like a deep well
That owes two buckets, filling one another,
The emptier ever dancing in the air,
The other down, unseen, and full of water.
That bucket down and full of tears am I,
Drinking my griefs whilst you mount up on high.   [IV i 183–8]

Thus the aim was, as Pasco put it, 'to reflect the similarities in the two men, rather than the opposites' (in 'A Pair of Kings', *Plays and Players*, June 1973, p. 27, quoted by Eileen Totten). Anne Righter's book, *Shakespeare and the Idea of the Play* (1961) showed the men as actually switching identities as one descended and the other rose. She writers of Richard's death: 'He and Bolingbroke have changed places once again; it is now the latter's turn to find himself in the position of the actor' ([Harmondsworth], p. 113). In the programme Righter wrote: 'Richard's journey from king to man is balanced by Bolingbroke's progress from a single to a twin-natured being. Both movements involve a gain and a loss. Each, in its own way, is tragic'. Bolingbroke's advance, however, is tragic only if he is unwillingly drawn into usurpation (which can just be derived from the text, and is just actable). Other parallels between them are more literal: the men are cousins, and both consolidate power through assassinations, with consequent civil strife.

Though Barton apparently directed both men in much the same way, the personalities of the actors and their own thinking produced radically different views of Richard and Bolingbroke.

Pasco's Richard was the more conventional reading of the part: the man with absolute belief in Divine Right, 'a sturdy, rather insensitive optimist' (Benedict Nightingale, *New Statesman*, 20 April 1973). Hence Richard is all the more crestfallen in defeat, till recovering a resilience in prison.

So Nightingale sees a contrast between the playing of the part by Pasco and Richardson thus: 'Pasco is an extravert, amply justifying the comparisons with the sun applied to him, and Richardson an introvert, understandably mistrusted by his barons'. Elaine Totten sees Richardson as unusually not wanting kingship: 'Pasco plays his king more as a Christ like figure, certain of his divine right . . . Richardson sees his King as a man who is delighted to be released from his dual role' (*Plays and Players*, June 1973, p. 28). J. W. Lambert brings out the different ways they react to their fall: 'Pasco's Richard, when the divinity that hedges a king is dissolved, is left an utterly wounded human being; Richardson's, when the regal mask is stripped away, reveals another mask beneath, and then another' (*Sunday Times*, 22 Sept. 1974). Richardson himself sees the contrast emerging most clearly in the final scene: 'Dickie plays the prison scene poetically, beautifully as a wounded martyr. I play it as a liberated human being who has at last discovered what it is to be real' (Totten, p. 28).

Though Richardson's king was nervous from the start, backing away from Bolingbroke as though in fear, he was completely savage in his wish that his enemies might find a lurking adder under every flower they plucked [III ii 19–22]. In the deposition scene, squatting at the king's feet suggesting a court fool, he sighed 'No' with half-humorous regret [200] but delivered his last line in anguish, 'Whither you will, so I were from your sights' [314].

Richardson has given a useful insight into the actor's art in explaining how he found the emotion of the deposition:

The Christmas before I did it my younger son, who was quite small, had asked for a train set and we got it and there was much excitement getting it working then something went wrong. He was a bit hamfisted and broke something irrevocably and it could not function again until it was mended. He picked it up and threw it – it struck the Christmas tree and was broken even more and I watched the tears pour down his face as he said, 'I don't want it any more; it's no good to me any more'. I was annoyed and pointed out how long he had waited for it and asked why he could not wait until it was repaired and he repeated, 'If it's broken, I don't want it any more' and suddenly, as actors do, I thought 'Good God, that's it, the Deposition Scene!' He throws away his crown and all the paraphernalia of monarchy in exactly the same way as my son throws away a train because it isn't fit to play with any more. It's been broken – it's been spoilt by chance, by ill-fortune, it's not of any use to me any more, and I had found my starting-point (*Shakespeare's Players*, [London, 1983], p. 52, quoted by Judith Cook.)

Richardson has described his approach to the part of Bolingbroke: 'I saw him as a young man who, in the early scenes, is very much under the influence of his glamorous cousin . . . In the early scenes leading up to his banishment he is at least as flowery, as poetic and lyrical in his imagery, as Richard. So here is a young man in awe and admiration of his cousin, and he gets this dreadful slap when he is first banished for ten years, then it is reduced to six years, and that makes him change:

> How long a time lies in one little word!
> Four lagging winters and four wanton springs
> End in a word – such is the breath of kings.   [I iii 213–15]

Now we all know from the Bible that people who go off into the wilderness come back changed. Bolingbroke comes back a quiet man, a man not prepared to push, a man who chooses well the sort of people who will do his pushing for him, a man waiting for the right moment to seize his chance, and can see that if the cards are played correctly, that chance is inevitable. Unlike Richard III, he has the patience to wait for the exact moment and, of course, it pays off. His tragedy is that having got it, he realises just what it is to be a medieval monarch and that was the way I played it. Out of that comes the necessity to kill Richard. It was inevitable, a political necessity.' But evil in the playing of Bolingbroke arises less from the character as written than from the demand for conflict in drama: Richardson 'felt he had to be played as something of a villain or otherwise Richard had nobody to bounce off' (Ibid., pp. 53–4). So Richardson's Bolingbroke began in injured innocence, then on his return from Brittany looked like 'a dapper young executive with his eyes on the key to the managing director's washroom' (Nightingale, *New Statesman*, 20 April 1973), yet ended tired, guilty and harassed.

Pasco's approach was unorthodox, an unambitious Bolingbroke. Pasco saw him as 'a plodder', which is plausible and as a 'countryman who could have been a successful country squire . . . against all the panache and panoply of power' (*Shakespeare's Players*, p. 53). Pasco played a most unlikely hero, usurper and murderer: this Bolingbroke was bewildered by the way the throne fell to him, then unsure about taking it.

An American critic missed this aspect of Pasco's interpretation while neatly contrasting the two performances: 'Richardson is cold and withdrawn; men would follow him because they want to ally themselves with his strength. Pasco is less impersonal, more sincere; a rebel men would follow out of trust' (Albert Bermel, *New Leader*, 18 Feb. 1974, p. 21).

Barton's version was the most remarkable – and best documented – of modern times.

8   STRATFORD FESTIVAL, ONTARIO: THREE ACTORS, DIRECTED ZOE CALDWELL, 1979

Stratford, Ontario, in 1979 featured three different Richards playing opposite three different Bolingbrokes. This was in part an opportunity missed, for had each played against three different actors, more might have been revealed. Unlike the RSC's venture, actors did not learn more about one role through 'inhabiting' their antagonist. This triple casting could be justified only as spreading the best parts around – and a few diligent audience members could see three ways of playing the roles. Casting and direction did not appear designed to show three contrasting interpretations; rather, as with Barton's production, differences emerged from the personalities of the actors. Nevertheless, the versions gave different answers to the issue of whether Bolingbroke ruthlessly seizes the throne or whether an ineffective Richard gives it up.

Stephen Russell's Richard was very weak and soft, with a Christ-like look. He was 'a passive, effete king who walks serenely, head aloft, and speaks in calm, measured tones. His capitulation is that of a man in despair, utterly discouraged that so many have turned against him. He simply gives up' (Lyle Slack, *Hamilton Spectator*, 15 June 1979). 'The king of elegy. The actor slips masterfully from the light intonation of unquestionable position to a gentle pathos, a pure weeping sorrow. It is a lyrical study and Russell's last warrior-like leap against death comes as a surprise. He flies into a moment of human fury' (Patricia Keeney Smith, 'Stratford: Daring if not Soaring', *Macleans's*, 25 June 1979, p. 47).

Nicholas Pennell was the most truly majestic Richard – proud, dominating, stately, morally strong. With these qualities went an aloofness, arrogance, a lack of humanity. Richard had too an occasional weakness for frivolity and an erratic streak. He depends only on words, 'madly making words work, using language – his only instrument of power – to explore and, hopelessly, explain' (Ibid.). The niceties of court involve him more than the duties of state. Yet he retains nobility throughout. 'In the case of Pennell, you figure he deserved what he got', concluded Slack. 'Maradan evokes more compassion: you sense a better man inside his Richard'.

Frank Maradan was the most compelling and distinctive of the three. He is very tall, thin, frail, arms hanging limply at his side, speaking in a kind of weepy chant. He shows sensuality, immaturity (a child playing at being king), aestheticism, 'a poet of decadence' (P. K. Smith) languishing in defeat. 'Maradan's eyes, like prunes floating in olive oil, epitomize the mind made shifty and shallow by corruption. This is a sly, silky, almost sinister Richard, redeemed, from time to time, by fleeting recoveries of virtues of which the king has been drained by fawning, self-seeking men' (MacKenzie Porter, *Toronto Sun*, 18 June 1979). 'Always, always there is the fey, sweet smile, a more-in-sorrow-than-in-anger air about his speeches. When he tells his followers "Go to Flint Castle. There I'll pine away" [III ii 209] you feel he's likely to do exactly that: maybe even before he gets to Flint Castle' (Audrey Ashley, *Ottawa Citizen*, 9 June 1979). 'Maradan, in his final scene alone in his cell, reminded one of nothing so much as Anthony Perkins in the final scene from *Psycho*. It was a scene displaying much relief at being deprived of any kind of self-will' (Richard Whelan, *Stratford Beacon-Herald*, 9 June 1979). Maradan's interpretation was rich but not contradictory, a man naive, weak and neurotic, with streaks of malevolence and aestheticism.

Of the three Bolingbrokes, Jim McQueen, opposed to

Maradan, was the most likeable and deserving. McQueen, as
Garebian noted, 'has the intensity and pitch of Sean Connery'.
A practical man, he looked the winner from his first
appearance, his ascent inevitable. Though understandably
cocky at times, he was graceful and relaxed, sympathetic
because of his open honest face.

Craig Dudley, challenging Russell, simply drove
remorselessly to achieve the throne. This Bolingbroke was
'a dashing super-politician, a performance engagingly
transparent in motivation' (Gina Mallett, *Toronto Star*, 11
June 1979). Dudley was also the most boyish of the three
Bolingbrokes, and was curiously uneasy and wavering in the
deposition scene.

Rod Beattie, set against Pennell, took the most unusual
approach, and was least convincing. Shrill and strident, he
was small, dark and bearded, suggesting a gypsy or, more
correctly, a Welshman. He disastrously lacked charisma and
it was hard to see him collecting followers in any cause.

With little movement, the few physical contacts were more
noticeable: at Flint Castle, saying 'We do debase ourselves,
cousin, do we not?' [III iii 127], Richard took Aumerle's hand
for comfort, and then Aumerle stealthily put his arm round
Richard's waist. Richard also gently put a hand on Bushy's
knee, while always keeping his distance from his Queen –
slight hints towards seeing Richard as homosexual.

Two minor performers – rarely mentioned for most
productions – stood out. Aumerle (Lorne Kennedy) was 'a
marvellous bantam cock of pride and loyalty to the king'.
The Duchess of York (Jessica Booker) 'displayed the
shameless passion of a mother for one of her progeny. Ms.
Booker is coyly endearing and heart rendingly sympathetic
at the same time. We laugh at her Duchess but underneath
lies the silent brook of truth which informs all she does'
(Richard Whelan, *Stratford Beacon-Herald*, 11 June 1979).

While *Richard II* has no comic subplot or funny characters,
some at least of the laughs in performance are intended by
the author. At Stratford, Ontario, the audience laughed at
such lines as Richard's 'Our doctors say this is no month to
bleed' [I i 157] and John of Gaunt's 'To God, the widow's
champion and defence' [I ii 43], and at the servant who

forgets to tell York of the Duchess's death, remembering as an afterthought [II ii 93–7]. The bumbling York's submission to Bolingbroke drew laughter for 'I do remain as neuter' and immediately after for 'So fare you well,/Unless you please to enter in the castle/And there repose you for this night' [II iii 158–60]. More curiously in this ritualistic production, the throwing down of gages in front of the new king was guyed, 'with much broad slapping of gloves, and at "Who sets me else?" [IV i 57] Aumerle looked as who should say "How many more?" At the news of Norfolk's death (98), all crossed themselves, and the effect was a stageful of people scratching their armpits in unison' (Ralph Berry, 'Stratford Festival, Canada', *Shakespeare Quarterly*, 31, Summer 1980, p. 169). Bolingbroke's reply, 'Sweet peace conduct his sweet soul to the bosom/Of good old Abraham!' [103–4], is also flippantly delivered to gain a laugh.

The director was Zoe Caldwell; 154 lines were cut. The reactions of the Duke and Duchess of York to Aumerle's plot (which is often judged badly-written and which may distract from Richard's fate at a crucial late stage in the play) passed by more quickly with 18½ lines removed from v ii and 27 more cut from v iii, including 9 of the 11 lines [101–9] of one of the Duchess's three pleas. Speeding the close, Percy's report of the death of the Abbot of Westminster and the exiling of the Bishop of Carlisle were cut [v vi 19–29]. Tiny verbal changes were made to aid comprehension (Willoughby's 'I wot not what', II i 250, became 'I *know* not what'; Bolingbroke's speech to York, 'Look on my wrongs with an indiffent eye' was altered to '*impartial* eye', II iii 115).

The stage was bare and austere, almost abstract. 'Daphne Dare's set design gave us largely an empty space divided by rectangles and straight lines in white, silver, and black. Nothing was allowed to interfere with the image of five long white steps with a thin silver throne atop the highest level. Downstage were low metal stools, one at either corner, and the throne stood against a rectilinear background of white panels that could be raised or lowered on cue. The economic set and decor were held in relief against a backdrop that was lit by different colours for different scenes,' pastel shades of rose and pale blue (Keith Garebian, 'The 1979 Stratford

Festival', *Journal of Canadian Studies*, 14, Winter 1979–80). Big sculptured silver trees floated in for a sparse garden scene. The tournament scene was brightened with banners, lifesize sculptured horses rolled in on tracks and dazzling shining armour.

Actors moved as little as possible and movements were rigidly symmetrical, with groupings often triangular. Some moves were purely pictorial. 'When in Act 4 the Bishop is arrested for treason [1. 150] and the Abbot of Westminster is told to take him off, they move from up right to down left, simply to match Aumerle, who moved earlier from up left to down right to answer Bagot's charges. Both times they cross in front of the King with their backs to him. Later, when Northumberland has stopped trying to get Richard to read his list of crimes [IV i 271] and has moved upstage with his back to the audience, Aumerle moves to an exactly equivalent position on the other side of the stage. Turning their backs on the King – God's substitute, his deputy, the anointed King – is not the only eccentricity the lords commit. They address him, or one another, through the backs of their heads in order to keep the picture right' (B. A. Young, *Financial Times*, 28 June 1979).

Such effects made the drama distant and artificial: 'The play is not so much acted as presented as a pageant', wrote B. A. Young. The intended effect was clear. Garebian was impressed: 'This stylization was a refreshingly original way of emphasizing Shakespeare's concern with what Tillyard calls "the proper disposition of things"'. Berry commented: 'The stylized postures and moves of the actors suggested a caste-bound society, locked into a form of collective unreality ... It takes a good actor to stand still, and some of the younger sort looked distinctly uncomfortable, as though they were playing statues and the music stopped at the wrong moment. Moreover, a courtier is by definition comfortable at a court; it's his *métier*' (p. 168). This austerity communicated a view of court life at the time and also forced attention to the spoken word, for meaning and for pure sound. Yet for most spectators the disadvantages were greater: life was frozen, so feeling and emotion were missing.

9 ROYAL SHAKESPEARE COMPANY, ALAN HOWARD, DIRECTED TERRY HANDS, 1980–81

The RSC's next *Richard II* after Barton's was directed by Terry Hands, who had a reputation for an operatic approach. He stated that the play 'is less a play, more a mass. A requiem mass. You mourn its going. Both men talk of pilgrimages and God as a court of appeal; thus testing the divinity of Kingship (as Richard does in his murder scene) is challenging God' (Robert Warden, 'All the King's Men', *Event*, 13 Nov. 1981). Hands added: 'Kings have been out of fashion for a long time. People are embarrassed by them. But our leaders still have almost divine power' (Lucy Hughes-Hallett, 'The Geometry of Necessity', *RSC Yearbook 1980–81*, p. 22).

An approach through the mass and divine power was in accord with elegiac music from Guy Wolfenden and a formal, imposing, stylised-medieval set by Farrah. Richard's court, said Farrah, presents 'the glory of the dying Gothic age: very bright, very elegant, full of gilded wood, like a medieval painting' (Ibid., p. 23). Farrah designed 'a rectangular floor, in gold, stretching from the forestage almost to the backcloth, with deeply marked lines lending perspective. 'The steeply raked back wall of the first scene is carved with huge emblems of the Christian King of Kings and his saints, enfolding the temporal king and his bishops, and in front of each panel stand the Bishop of Carlisle, Richard II and John of Gaunt. For the tournament scene [I iii] the wall tilts back, its descending top becoming a horizon over which, at the back of the stage, rises the sun of Richard in his golden throne, accompanied by the deep reds and blues of his royal standards' (Julie Hankey, *Times Literary Supplement*, 14 Nov. 1980). Richard's descent at Flint Castle was made down this steeply sloping wall. The huge picture of Richard at the back was finally lowered to make a sloping floor, enabling Bolingbroke to stand on the face of his defeated rival. David Suchet pointed out that, similarly, priests in ancient Egypt would symbolically tread on the face of deposed monarchs.

For costumes, Richard and his followers began in gold with Bolingbroke and his supporters in dark colours, so that when power shifts, it is, in Farrah's words, 'as though a crow is taking over from a dove'.

Richard II was staged at the same time as *Richard III*, Alan Howard playing both title roles. The two plays had very little in common: the point was the total contrast between the divine right of the second Richard and the crude power of the third. Howard commented that '*Richard II* is a writer's play; *Richard III* is an actor's play' (Hughes-Hallett, p. 23). Cushman added another neat contrast: 'R2 loves his own image, R3 hates it' (*The Observer*, 9 Nov. 1980).

Alan Howard's playing of Richard is best summed up as a man outwardly supremely confident and inwardly insecure, expressed in actions and words that are playful and capricious. This Richard, explains Robert Cushman, 'regards kingship as a license to say and do outrageous, even meaningless things, and get applauded for them, but is cripplingly uncertain as to whether he can carry it off. This Richard insults Gaunt on his death-bed as if he were doing a turn, then turns to Bushy, Bagot and company apparently asking "Didn't I do well?" The nervousness betrays him. Before he has said a word, we see him in this production trying on his crown with an expression of fascinated distaste; plainly he is not getting job-satisfaction but he also sees no prospects in alternative employment. Then he turns to confront an impassive row of courtiers' (*The Observer*, 15 Nov. 1981). With Mowbray and Bolingbroke in I i and I iii, he half-hides contempt of both under his raillery, sarcastically emphasising 'We shall see/Justice design the victor's *chivalry*' [I i 202–3]. John Barber saw at the start Richard blindly in love with being king: Richard is 'infatuated and not only with the applause he so shamelessly solicits from his toadies. He is infatuated with the panoply of his office, with his dandyish apparel and, above all, with the idea that he is divine' (*Daily Telegraph*, 11 Nov. 1981).

This appeared as scene-by-scene playing, an 'existential' approach, to Billington; 'He is a monarch who seems to define himself anew with each scene. At first, he is all anointed holiness full of saintly smiles and tapering, prayerful hands. In the lists at Coventry, he becomes a quivering ceremonial figure, troubled in ermine and velour. But later Mr. Howard is rash, fierce, impetuous, frivolous, crying "We will ourself in person to this war" [I iv 42] even as he tries on a new frock in front of the mirror [a sign of vanity anticipating Richard's big scene with a mirror at his deposition and previously used by Barton]. Inevitably in defeat he acquires the dignity of pathos, but even here you feel Mr. Howard's Richard is a man assuming new roles so that he turns up for the Westminster deposition scene as Jesus Christ in a white robe [see Plate 5]. But the greatest sadness is reserved for Pomfret prison where, shorn and defrocked, he tries to reconstruct his personality and finds he cannot even talk to his groom' (*The Guardian*, 11 Nov. 1981).

The key to the performance for Irving Wardle was the contrast between Richard in public and Richard in private. 'Let me offer a typical contrast between the two. In the opening scene, he delivers his opinion on the two challengers straight out to the house; then shuts his eyes on us. The King has briefly taken us into his confidence, and now the audience is at an end. Set that against his row with the dying Gaunt. Mr. Howard seems to explode in ungovernable fury, his voice cracking round the old man like a bullwhip; then, without a pause, he turns to his private group of cronies, all smiles, for their applause at his performance. Until we find him, mortified into self-knowledge in the Pomfret cell, he is invariably surrounded by an audience, with whom he takes the king-actor metaphor to the limit' (*The Times*, 11 Nov. 1981). James Fenton saw Richard's extremes less as public/private than as triumph/disaster: 'Howard displays an hysterical bifurcation: on the one hand, all is well, and nothing can stand in the way of royal good fortune; on the other hand, all is lost. There is no intervening mood . . . The court must either be utterly splendid or it is nothing' (*Sunday Times*, 9 Nov. 1980).

While Richard certainly alternates between public and informal occasions, usually he is viewed as one man before his downfall and virtually another after. Howard 'goes through most of the first half with a fixed, superior smile which would have provoked a saintlier man than Bolingbroke.

Facing disaster, his smile does not vanish, it becomes manic instead. He delivers his great lilting monologues as if they belonged to someone else. As he shuffles in his white gown among the black-uniformed dukes his whole manner is that of a lunatic with delusions of grandeur rather than a king with intimations of mortality' (Christopher Hudson, *News Standard*, 4 Nov. 1980). Wardle identifies not just change but maturity in the later Richard, who has changed from 'sarcastic bully' to 'subtle ironist'.

Some found fault with Howard's speaking of the verse: 'At the great speeches, his gravelly voice either rises to a high note and stays there, or it describes an aria where the inflections are chosen for their music rather than their sense' (B. A. Young, *Financial Times*, 4 Nov. 1980). Wardle noted a speech where Howard chose sense over verse: '"What must the King do now?" [III iii 143] is delivered in a terrified gabble. He really wants to know. It is the panic-stricken demand of an actor who has forgotten his lines' (*The Times*, 4 Nov. 1980).

For Bolingbroke, Terry Hands gave this clue; 'Bolingbroke is the manager of the future. He breaks away from the dictates of medievalism – an England manager rather than King' (Robert Warden, *Event*). The actor, David Suchet, adds his approach: the man 'is a bluff soldier unused to court language and badinage. What he gets (but does not expect) is a moment of total humiliation' in the deposition scene. 'For the first time, as Bolingbroke sets the crown on his head, he suddenly realises that he doesn't want it – not one little bit' (Richard Edmonds, *Birmingham Post*, 29 Nov. 1980).

Suchet's Bolingbroke has two turning points. Ambition dawns on him as he is exiled: he realises 'Such is the breath of kings' [I iii 215]. He sends an ultimatum to Richard 'beginning grandiloquently with his own name: "Henry Bolingbroke" [III iii 35] – here Mr. Suchet breaks off for a moment [the half-line in the text encourages a pause here], bemused and excited (Hark at me, I'm talking royal). He has found himself' (Robert Cushman, *The Observer*, 15 Nov. 1981). At Flint he maintains a brooding, controlled presence. Then Richard outmanoeuvres him to hold centrestage during the deposition, loading Bolingbroke with the regalia and thrusting him on to the throne. At once Bolingbroke wonders whether he was right to want the crown.

When next seen, he works at a desk, wearing a greatcoat, with spectacles and a little grey beard. As king, he has become careworn and introspective. He is stunned by the stresses and responsibilities, sounding dazed as he prounces: 'Thy pains, Fitzwater, shall not be forgot./Right noble is thy merit, well I wot' [v vi 17–18].

The small part of the Queen had an unusually strong impact: 'Domini Blythe, her long fair hair halfway down her back, is a moving Queen, who never allows her sadness to overcome her self-possession. Her torch-lit farewell as the King is taken to Pomfret is beautiful' (B. A. Young).

That John of Gaunt died looking strong and healthy may have been less miscasting than part of Hands' conception of the drama. Sheridan Morley saw this and disliked it: 'Instead of the usual craggy dying prophet, new-inspired with a glimpse of England's collapse, we have a Tito Gobbi lookalike booming out the lines in rotund good health and then suddenly dropping off in the most unlikely death since Little Nell's. Gaunt is apparently playing at being old and ill in much the same way that Richard is playing at being King; the performance is all' (*Shooting Stars*, [London, 1983], pp. 246–7).

If the key to Hands' production was a requiem mass, the number of comic touches was unexpected. Richard and his cronies smirk when Gaunt's wealth is seized [II i 160], then Richard cups his ear towards York, knowing an outburst is inevitable. The Gardeners obliquely mock the Queen, defying both plausibility and the text. York tugging his boots from under his wife's feet added to the fun of v ii; surprisingly, though, his impatient efforts to take a ring off have the audience laughing when the Servingman tells him that the Duchess of Gloucester has died [II ii 97]. On the other hand spectators were held silent while all the gages were flung down in quick succession at the beginning of IV i.

Hands' insights included grasping the precise meaning of the text when Richard says to John of Gaunt: 'Thy son is banished upon good advice/Whereto thy tongue a party-verdict gave' [I iii 233–4]. Bolingbroke is astonished to hear

that his father supported sending him to exile. Hands showed
Bolingbroke's ambition to possess the earth of Britain by
having him stride up and down outside Flint Castle. In a
fine foreshadowing touch, Bolingbroke in IV i offers the crown
to Northumberland to carry, then thinks better of it.

Hands had some good visual effects, though the dispersing
Welshmen singing as they walked backwards into darkness
in II iv were merely operatic. Richard, leaving after the
deposition, snatched a blue handkerchief from Aumerle and
strode out hiding his face, still an actor with an eye to effect.
Exton was accompanied by nine murderers, (the figure comes
from Holinshed, which reviewers missed!), then the close
gave the 'sensation of a kingdom dissolving into chaos as
black-clad messengers burst in from fiery darkness' (Michael
Billington, *The Guardian*, 11 Nov. 1981).

Finally, this version was not just a star turn as Richard.
Crucially, 'the Middle Ages wane before our eyes. Expediency
and pragmatism replace a somewhat decadent chivalry. The
nation stumbles, then appears to recover. The Wars of the
Roses loom, dimly perceived by the many and more sharply
by the new. This is what history-lessons should have been
like: pulsating, immediate, sucking you into the march of
events and holding you there' (Benedict Nightingale, *New
Statesman*, 20 Nov. 1981).

10 THÉÂTRE DU SOLEIL,
DIRECTED ARIANE MNOUCHKINE, 1982–84

British theatregoers have grown accustomed to changes of
time and place in productions of many of Shakespeare's
plays, from *Othello* and *Troilus and Cressida* set in the Crimean
War, to *Much Ado* placed in 19th-century India, to *Measure for
Measure* on an island in the Caribbean after World War II.
English directors, however, rarely feel able to treat English
history in ways that are disrespectful, even if highly
imaginative: one exception for *Richard II* was its transfer to
Russia in 1917, noted in Part One. It was a French director,

Ariane Mnouchkine with her Théâtre du Soleil, who in 1982 offered a greatly transformed *Richard*, first at Vincennes, a Paris suburb, then at the Avignon Festival and in 1984 in Los Angeles for the Olympic Games.

Mnouchkine, wrote James Fenton, had found a new starting point for a production of Shakespeare: 'If you ask yourself what is the major artistic principle behind English productions of Shakespeare, the answer surely must be: they seek to draw the experience depicted in the plays as close as possible to our own. This is a fine idea but it is not the only possible approach. Suppose you start with the opposite intention. You say, Shakespeare is not our contemporary, his characters belong to the heroic past, they do not live according to the same rules by which we live, they do not speak in the same way in which we speak. To follow such thoughts to their logical conclusion is to demand a style of production unmistakably different from our own, rich tradition' (*You Were Marvellous*, [London, 1983], p. 256).

This was Mnouchkine's own explanation of her approach: 'The history plays are about ritual, about divine legitimacy. Western theater doesn't have a form to depict this. It only has one convention: realism. And I'm convinced that Shakespeare can't be played realistically. Do you really think that when Henry IV appeared in public ceremonies, he walked like everybody else? Japanese theater is the only one that has a ritual. The Oriental actor, using masks, signs, dances, songs and everything else, shows what's going on inside him. He doesn't try to hide his emotions, like most actors in the West have been doing for the past 30 years. Besides, theater is a metaphor, and Shakespeare a poet of perpetual metaphor . . . The role of theater and of the actor is to make flower what is buried. Realism makes nothing flower. Realism hides what is already hidden'. Apart from this choice of ritual over realism, Mnouchkine makes a distinct approach to the language, translating the play herself: 'Shakespeare's language is so dense and imaginative that it becomes a form of stimulation for the audience, like a caress or something close to carnal' (Anne Tremblay, 'A French Director Gives Shakespeare a New Look', *New York Times*, 10 June 1984, Section II, pp. 6, 14).

Mnouchkine's inspiration was kabuki. Actors ran along the lengthy runways to the big stage; surfaces were covered in coconut matting. Silk backdrops were changed to reflect mood; the few props included black-lacquered stools, green plants for the garden and a prison like a pagoda. Oriental percussion music accompanied. Actors, wearing Japanese robes with Elizabethan ruffs, faced the audience with knees flexed and elbows turned out. Speeches were shouted, clearly and unemotionally. Although Aumerle's conspiracy in v ii and iii was cut, the version lasted nearly five hours. 'Productions were characterized by remarkable gestural precision and the inscription of balletic patterns in clearly delimited spaces. In Act i i of *Richard II*, for example, each of the assembled nobles had his own set of movements, swaying up and down to a particular inner rhythm, striking out with his arms and cocking his head in a designated time sequence. Every staccato displacement defined an emotional leap in response to Bolingbroke's accusations. The overall choreographic design, in *Richard II* especially, evoked the horizontality and verticality of a chess game. In certain scenes, such as the confrontation on the battleground (*Richard II*, iii iii) the result was breathtaking; the actors-turned-centaurs, ribbon crops in hand and aligned in spatial zones, pranced, paraded and excitedly bumped into each other. Of them all only Percy, foreshadowing *Henry IV*, could not control his high-strung, high-stepping horse from breaking rank' (Judith G. Miller, *Theatre Journal*, March 1983, p. 116). At the end, Exton lays out the body of Richard under the low table which has served as a throne and the tired King Henry stretches out above the corpse, suggesting a double tomb.

The effect of this extraordinary treatment of the play, Fenton concluded, 'is to redeem those qualities of the play which one might, unconsciously, have made allowance for. The formality of the play's constructions is revealed. The argument develops like a terrific algebra, a vast equation whose terms must be shifted and juggled around, according to mysteriously beautiful rules, in order to arrive at the meaning of the term kingship' (*You Were Marvellous*, p. 257). Most saw the distant medieval world newly distanced by

the Japanese setting, bringing out especially the ritual so
prominent in the drama.

11 CONCLUSION

Studying recent productions of *Richard II* leads to the
following conditions:

1. Richard is inescapably the key character. Compared
with Hamlet (as he has been since W. B. Yeats called him
'an unripened Hamlet'), scope for different approaches is
very limited. In recent years to the poet-king were added the
actor-king, very aware of playing a role to an audience, and
the philosopher-king, accepting loss of the throne and gaining
self-knowledge in prison.

2. New attempts have been made to give Bolingbroke
almost as much importance as Richard, e.g. added lines in
1973; attention focused on the part in 1973 and 1979.

3. Bolingbroke shown to be stressed, tired, ageing, unhappy
once he is king.

4. Attempts to find hidden depths in such other parts as
York, Aumerle, the Queen and the Duchess of Gloucester
have scarcely succeeded. Northumberland as a sinister power-
behind-the-throne has, however, added new weight to this
part.

5. When *Richard II* is interpreted as the first of a series of
four histories, Richard's fall leads directly to later disasters
and represents the end of the Middle Ages. This approach
gives added importance to Northumberland and perhaps to
Percy and the Welsh Captain (if he is Glendower of *Henry
IV*).

6. New thinking (e.g. on the King's two bodies and on the
work as self-consciously a theatre piece) influences directorial
thinking and may be reflected in performance.

7. The political dimension – the nature of rulers and the
justification of rebellion – has had new attention, reacting
against the subject being merely the tragedy of the poet-king.
This presents difficulties, as monarchs are not prominent in

late 20th-century political thought and divine right is a wholly alien concept.

8. Stress on ritual, formality, even 'the mass', as in the gold-robed figures like brasses on tombs in 1980 and the stark sets of 1973 and 1979.

Shakespeare's histories have not often been drastically rethought in recent stagings. Could a production exploit the blood-in-a-garden image pattern? Could the suffering, silent peasants and foot soldiers play more part? Could the three periods of the action (1398–99), the writer (1595) and the present 1980s all be there, as air-raid sirens, robes over modern dress, rifles and swords brought the present to the National Theatre's *Coriolanus* in 1984? What can be emphasised apart from poetry and/or ritual?

When I began seriously studying this play, I saw it as about Richard, a man whose tragedy was that he had to cope with all the problems of being king in a turbulent era. I also had a sense of the *sound* of Richard and of the verse, echoes of Gielgud in my head. Close attention to the play soon made Bolingbroke and York also intriguing characterisations. Gradually I discovered the art of the structuring: words (I became sensitive to every use and nuance of 'time' and 'blood'); themes (first one king and then his successor have to respond to similar problems); and visually (enthroned kings, angry men, gages thrown down, kneeling and refusal to kneel). Most of all, I saw the drama's exploration of such practical issues of politics as trust vs mistrust and leniency vs severity.

READING LIST

The text quoted here is the New Penguin, ed. Stanley Wells (Harmondsworth, 1969). The other two major modern editions are the Arden, ed. Peter Ure (Methuen, London, 1956) and the New Cambridge, ed. Andrew Gurr (1984), with substantial introductions. Gurr's footnotes cover many of the important journal articles. The Arden and New Cambridge editions include excerpts from Holinshed and Daniel's poem, 'The Civil Wars'. Three other editions merit a mention: the BBC Television Shakespeare, ed. John Wilders (London, 1978); the Macmillan, with full facing-page notes and a sound introduction by Richard Adams (London, 1975); and the Signet, ed. Kenneth Muir, with an excerpt from Holinshed and three critical essays (New English Library, London, 1963).

Serious students should consult the New Variorum edition by Matthew W. Black (Philadelphia, Lippincott for the Modern Language Association of America, 1955). The text is the First Folio, while all the above editions are based on the First Quarto. Black has 352 pages of text and commentary, nearly 200 pages on date, dramatic time, stage history and so on and 100 pages of Sources.

SECONDARY SOURCES

The Macmillan *Casebook* on the play, edited by Nicholas Brooke (London, 1973), has excerpts from ten 'earlier critics' and eleven more recent essays.

A. R. Humphreys *Richard II* (Arnold: Studies in England Literature, 1967) surveys the play in 60 pages; Gareth Lloyd Evans introduces it briefly in Chapter 2 of Volume 2 of his *Shakespeare* (Oliver & Boyd, Edinburgh, 1969). Paul Johnson and Ian Richardson comment in *Shakespeare in Perspective*, I, ed. Roger Sales (London, 1982).

The basis account of Tudor views of history as reflected in the plays remains *Shakespeare's History Plays*, by E. M. W. Tillyard (Chatto & Windus, London, 1944).

Tillyard has been comprehensively challenged in recent years (Was there an orthodox Tudor view? Or more than one view? Did Shakespeare reflect an existing view or think independently? Is the subject much more personal relationships than interpretation of history? Is *Richard II* significantly the first of a tetralogy?) See:

Graham Holderness, *Shakespeare's History* (Gill and Macmillan, 1985)

H. A. Kelly, *Divine Providence in the England of Shakespeare's Histories* (Harvard U.P., Cambridge, Mass., 1970)

Robert Orstein, *A Kingdom for a Stage* (Harvard U.P., Cambridge, Mass., 1972)

Wilbur Sanders, *The Dramatist and the Received Idea* (Cambridge, 1968)
S. C. Sen Gupta, *Shakespeare's Historical Plays* (Oxford U.P., London, 1964)
John Wilders, *The Lost Garden* (Macmillan, London, 1978) (Wilders also
helpfully compares the histories with Shakespeare's Roman plays)
James Winny, *The Player King* (Chatto & Windus, London, 1968).

Irving Ribner provides an overview of the form in *The English History Play in
the Age of Shakespeare* (revised edn, Barnes & Noble, New York, 1965).

John Baxter's *Shakespeare's Poetic Styles* (Routledge, London, 1980) is mainly
devoted to *Richard II*. G. R. Hibbard's *The Making of Shakespeare's Dramatic
Poetry* (Un. of Toronto P., 1981) and M. M. Mahood's *Shakespeare's Wordplay*
(Methuen, London, 1957) (Ch. 3) are also useful on this topic.

J. L. Styan discusses the effect of the plays on stage in *Shakespeare's Stagecraft*
(Cambridge U.P., 1967) and John Russell Brown's *Shakespeare Plays in
Performance* (Arnold, London, 1966) also reflects recent performance-based
approaches. For particular productions (apart from sources mentioned in Part
Two) see J. Dover Wilson and T. C. Worsley, *Shakespeare's Histories at Stratford,
1951* (Theatre Arts, New York, 1952) and A. C. Sprague, *Shakespeare's
Histories: Plays for the Stage* (Society for Theatre Research, London, 1964).

INDEX OF NAMES